BUILDING THE FUTURE TODAY

by John C. Clem

Trio Publications/Wichita, KS
www.triopubs.com

Library of Congress Catalog Card Number: 00-192787

ISBN 0-9678620-0-0

Author: Clem, John C.
Title: Building The Future Today: A guide to building products and methods for
              the new millennium
Edition: 1st edition
              Includes Index.

Printed in the United States on recycled content paper stock
01   10 9 8 7 6 5 4 3 2 1

Body printed on a **Xerox DocuTech 65 Digital Publisher**

Cover printed on a **Xerox DocuColor 2060 Digital Color Press**

For additional copies of this book, sales inquiries, special pricing for bulk
quantities, review copies, author interviews, general information on Trio
Publications, or other publicity information, please contact our sales department via e-mail at sales@triopubs.com

Published by Trio Publications
3238 English St.
Wichita, KS 67218

This book is dedicated to:

My wonderful wife, Dana,

without her support and encouragement,

this book would never exist

TABLE OF CONTENTS

Every day, people build new homes. These are new homes for first time homebuyers, new homes for growing families, and new homes for parents whose children have moved into their own homes. As our population grows we will continue to need and build new homes.

Beyond the basic functions of any home, we all have definite requirements in a home. These requirements change as our population increases and ages. These requirements also change as our environment changes, and our access to raw materials and fuels change. As we use our supply of raw building materials, the supply of these materials diminishes, and we must alter our building practices or seek alternative materials. Likewise, as we use our fuel resources, the supply of these fuel resources will diminish. As our supplies of building materials and fuels decrease, the cost of these items will increase. This trend of diminishing supplies and increasing costs can be seen today in both building materials and fuels. We have recently seen a significant increase in heating and automobile fuel costs. These cost increases may continue indefinitely. One solution to these diminishing supplies and increasing costs is to build more efficient homes.

Can we build better homes? Can we provide shelter for ourselves and protect the environment at the same time? Can this be done efficiently? Can we improve on current construction methods? Can we build homes that conserve energy? Can we make better use of the resources we have? Yes! We can build safe, secure, comfortable, beautiful, energy efficient, environmentally friendly homes. We have the materials and the knowledge to accomplish all of these things and more. We need to change some of our habits and methods to accomplish these goals. Is this practical? Yes! It is practical if we rethink how our homes are designed and built.

Building practices and material choices affect the quality of all the homes we build. At issue is a lack of concern for the environment in how the building materials directly, and indirectly, impact the environment. There are other construction methods and materials available, some of which can be more effective and efficient than traditional methods. Many progressive contractors are willing to try new methods of construction. They see benefits in not only how the home performs, but also in the positive way their companies are viewed by the general public, and by prospective homebuyers.

By educating people, and providing them with alternative, more effective building methods and ideas, a home can be designed and built that meet the owners needs while achieving other goals. Goals like conserving resources and reducing energy usage, building homes that last longer, are more comfortable, and increasing the use of recycled materials in home construction.

The general purpose of this book is to provide information about building materials, the environmental impact of those materials, improvements to existing construction methods, alternative construction methods, information about effective insulation methods, and the benefits of utilizing passive solar heating. Using better building practices can greatly improve the sustainability of our homes, reducing our impact on the environment. Many of these changes cost very little if anything to implement during home construction.

If we utilize even some of the information contained in this book as we build our homes, we can help to preserve our planet for future generations, and provide a better place in which our families can live and grow today.

BUILDING THE FUTURE TODAY

by John C. Clem

Trio Publications/Wichita, KS
www.triopubs.com

1   The Basics

Your home is supposed to provide you with protection and shelter, a place to raise your family, and a calm/stable space away from our crazy world. Many homes built today do not provide us with these things, because they are poorly constructed, poorly designed, and many times are built only to impress our peers. They do not take advantage of their location or their orientation to the sun, and many homes may also ignore some other basic functions that the home is supposed to provide.

Home: "1. A place where one lives; residence. 2. A house. 3. A dwelling place together with the family that lives there. 4. A place of origin."
--The American Heritage Dictionary

There are many elements that are combined to create a home. These elements range from the most minuscule item, such as a doorknob, to the all-encompassing house plan itself. These elements can be combined to make a successful home, or to create a disjointed structure with no flow or sense of harmony.

A successful home will combine all the elements of its construction with a defining purpose. The occupants, and their life-style define that purpose. Their life-style is defined by their personalities. The successful home is built to compliment those personalities.

Homes come in many shapes and sizes

There are seven basic principles, which should guide the design of any home:

Build to suit your needs
Build within your budget
Build to last
Build to preserve the environment
Build for energy efficiency
Build a healthy home
Build a safe home

These principles lead to questions that help to define the purpose of the home. For each of these principles, you must examine your feelings, needs, and requirements in a home. These questions will lead you to produce a list of items that you want to incorporate into your home, as well as a list of things that you want to avoid in your home. Through this self-analysis process, you will discover your true home needs.

3

Build to Suit Your Needs

Building a home to suit your needs. This is a simple principle, but do people really take a good look at their current needs, and future needs when they build a home? If you analyze your present and future needs, you can have a home that will better accommodate you, your family, and your budget.

How much home do you need today?
How much home will you need in 5 or 10 years?
How will the rooms in your home be used?
Who will use those rooms?
What areas should be next to each other?
What areas should be separated from one another?
What architectural features do you want in your home?
What conveniences do you want in your home?
Is your home suited for its surroundings?
What external influences do you want the home to enhance, or hide?

These are just a few of many questions you should ask yourself if you plan to build a home. There is a more complete list of questions in Appendix A, in the back of this book. There is also an electronic version (Microsoft Excel®) on our web site, www.futurehomestoday.com. Use this form to as you go through the process of planning your next home.

How much home do
you really need?
How much home can
you afford?

When it comes to a home, bigger isn't necessarily better. We all would like to have more home at some point in our lives, but how much home do we really need? Do you really need 4 bedrooms, and 3 baths today? What will the situation be 5 or 10 years from now? Many people get caught in the trap of wanting more home than they actually need or can afford. This is human nature. Many homes built today have only simple finishes, and offer an

atmosphere that lacks warmth, because they are designed with maximum size, and not comfort in mind. Often, this lack of detail is a result of budget constraints. Since the 1950's, the average family size has decreased, while the square footage per person in a home has almost tripled. Do we need all of this space, and can we use this space more efficiently?

How much space do we really need in a home? Are the formal dining and living rooms necessary with our life-styles today? How many people do you know who have these rooms, and rarely or never use them?

It is important to identify your home needs. Start by creating a list of rooms in your ideal home, and call this your "Needs List". You can divide this list into two halves, the "must have" side, and the "would like to have" side. On the "must have" side, list the rooms you absolutely cannot do without, such as the kitchen, family room, laundry room, etc. If you plan to work out of your home, a home office is probably a necessity. On the "would like to have" side, list the rooms you would like if your budget allows. These might be a home theater, guest bedroom, screened porch, greenhouse, etc.

This exercise will help you to understand what you really need in a home, and what you can add if there is enough money in your budget. This may also make you think about how the rooms in your home will be used. Many people visualize their future home, and how they would like to use the home. The problem is that most people have a difficult time separating their actual needs from the fantasy of their ideal home. The fantasy is fine, but you have to be able to pay for the fantasy.

Create a "Needs List" to help define the spaces in your future home

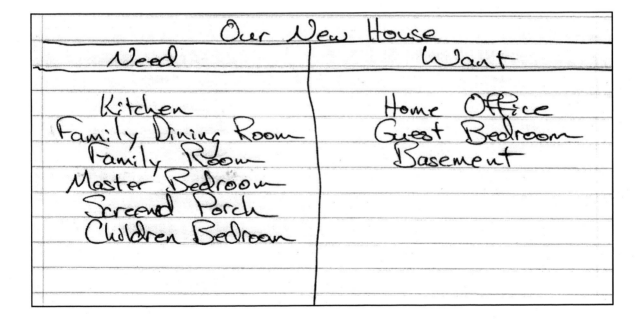

Look at how often you entertain friends or family as an example. How often do you really expect to have a group of friends or family over to your home, with a group of 15 people or more? Will you have this number of people over more than three or four times in any given year, during times when you cannot use outdoor areas? Most people will say no to this question, yet they visualize a large living area with the ability to accommodate groups of people.

Unfortunately, there is a cost involved with having this large living area for entertaining. Square footage costs money. Can you afford to invest the extra funds into your home for this purpose? You must realize that you will be entertaining people for less than 1% of the time you spend at home. Would you be better designing your living space so that you could rearrange some furniture in order to accommodate groups or parties? There are many possibilities.

We need to rethink how our homes are designed and built. We need to cast off the shackles of tradition, take a clean look at our real needs, and build our homes to suit those needs. Only this will make our homes more livable, comfortable, and affordable.

In homes, there are public and private spaces. Public spaces are those where the family spends the most time, such as the family room, kitchen, dining room, etc. A home also needs private spaces. Private spaces are those that are not normally used by everyone in the family, such as the parent's bedroom, or bathroom. People need private spaces to escape, and to be alone. We all need solitude from time to time, in order to allow our minds to settle, and to allow us

Comfortable, public areas are very important to any home

reflect upon the days events. The private space does not have to be totally separated from the rest of the home; it only needs to be a room that is separated from the normal flow of traffic and noise. This allows the normal activities of the home to continue without intruding upon another family member's quiet time.

You should also look at your family situation today, and what it will be in 5, 10, or 15 years. Have you chosen the town where you want to raise your children? If your children are older, and about to enter high school or college, you may not need a large home in a few years. You may be able to deal with a smaller home for a short time in anticipation of your children leaving for college, or starting their own homes. If your children are young or newborn, the nursery today may become the den of tomorrow. Think about the future, and how you might best utilize the space available. This process will often lead you to a home design, which is optimized to your current family situation, yet can be adapted as your family changes.

The style of homes has changed somewhat in the past 50 years. Many of today's designs will have the kitchen open to the dinning/family room. No longer is it a sequestered area used exclusively for preparing the family meals. The kitchen has even become the focal point of many modern homes. How often have your attended holiday gatherings where most of the guests are congregating in the kitchen? The downside to this design is that the kitchen needs to be kept in a fairly clean state on a consistent basis. It can be designed with a dividing counter set higher than the sink, which can help to hide dishes

Kitchens today are large and open to other living areas

not yet cleaned. An integrated breakfast bar can also provide an eating area for some or all of the family, helping to combine the family dining area with the kitchen. The breakfast bar can also serve double duty as a buffet serving area when entertaining family or friends.

Another consideration is comfort. What makes a home comfortable? There are many things that help to make a home comfortable. The size of the spaces can create a comfortable feeling. The furnishings in a home can greatly affect the comfort of the home, even the finish materials (floors, wall coverings, trim/woodwork, etc.) add to the comfort of a room.

What naturally feels more comfortable, a large room, or a small room? Most people will say the small room. For some reason, people like smaller, more confining spaces when they desire solitude. Smaller rooms create that cozy feeling. Adding a small private space off of a large family room or the master bedroom can be easy and efficient. Alcoves and window seats are examples of small, cozy spaces. These spaces can be designed or arranged to provide some separation from the rest of the family area, without being too removed from the activities of the home. These spaces can also add impact and interest to a room. What about making the space under the stairs larger, or more useful? There are many places where you can find spaces for this type of function, include one or several in your home design.

The materials used in the construction of the home can also add to how comfortable the home feels. Generally, natural materials create a more comfortable feeling. Examples are natural wood trim, or hardwood flooring. If your budget allows, incorporating wood into the interior of your home will be a plus. This not only will increase the value of your home, but it will also add to the comfort and beauty of the home. The materials used to finish your walls also affect the comfort level of your home. Finishes that are too smooth, and lack softness are not very inviting, where as materials that have an irregular texture, create shadows, and have depth will help to make the home feel more comfortable. This is a basic, but important characteristic to understand.

Furnishings are another factor in creating a comfortable room. Large, solid, over-stuffed furniture will be more comfortable than delicate, fancy furniture. Most people are attracted to large, soft pieces of furniture. Furniture that incorporates the richness and beauty of natural wood is a bonus, because they can help to tie the furniture into the rest of a room. The types of furniture you choose will even influence how guests will act in your home. If you have delicate, fancy furniture in your home, your guests may feel uncomfortable, because it is not comfortable to sit in, and the furniture does not allow your guests to relax. Large, soft furniture will be much more relaxing and inviting. This can greatly improve how your guests feel in your home. The color and texture of the furniture add to the effect.

Combining the formal and informal living spaces is efficient and cost effective

Can you make rooms serve a double duty? Having spaces that you can use for two or more functions creates a more efficient design, and allows you to splurge on other items in your home. Floor space costs money. By making the square footage of your home more efficient, you can use the money initially saved to upgrade the finishes in your home, or to add additional rooms to your home. Many people purchase homes that are simply finished on the interior, because they were buying square footage, and could not afford to add more expensive interior finishes to the home. Take the formal dining room for instance. Most people rarely use a formal dining room. How much money does a room you rarely use cost? Can you eliminate the formal dining room from your house plan, and upgrade the size and quality of the family

dining area? By improving the quality of the family dining area, you can make it serve the dual function of formal, and casual dining areas, while improving the overall comfort and quality of the home. This is an example of how you can reduce the size of your home, while increasing its quality, comfort, efficiency, and cost efficiency.

What kind of life-style does your family have? Do you like deep solitude, lots of interaction, or something in-between? Do you require peace and quiet to unwind after a hectic day? These things should be considered when deciding what type and style of the home you intend to build. A home must be able to function with all of the occupants, and their activities. The life-style of your family is tied closely with your needs list for a home. A home can be designed to compliment your life-style, or can be inadvertently designed to hinder your life-style.

A well designed room can serve the family and accomidate groups

If you do entertain often, you might consider designing your home with an emphasis on the public spaces, while minimizing the size of the private spaces. This can be accomplished by making the public spaces larger, adjacent to one another, and possibly separated by furniture that can be easily rearranged when needed. You could also design your home with an emphasis on the private spaces. Here you can spend the majority of your budget on the bedrooms and baths, while minimizing the more public kitchen and family room. Most people want a balance somewhere in-between these two extremes.

Many homes built today are open in design, and they also try to combine interior and exterior spaces into a larger living area. A deck/patio or screened porch can be placed next to one or more of the public family areas. This allows the family to move between these areas in times of moderate weather, and greatly expands the size of the home when entertaining during moderate weather. This type of arrangement expands the living area of the home, and is common today. These outdoor spaces are also important if you have children.

If you have small children, you will want areas where they can play (both inside and outside), yet still be within earshot or sight. An open design with an adjacent outdoor space, and a secure back yard is an ideal configuration. This allows the children to play indoors and out, while staying in close proximity to you. This arrangement can also help to increase the safety and security of your children. If your children are teenagers, you may still want the same features, with the addition of some spaces for study and privacy. A basement family room can serve both of these purposes.

As you age, your mobility will decrease. You may also find the need to have a disabled person live with you at some time. You can design your home so that it is easier for a person with a mobility problem, yourself or a relative, to move within. Reducing elevation changes inside the home is a good place to start. As you age, it becomes more difficult to climb up and down stairs. Reducing or eliminating stairs in the home will improve ease of movement. Would you want to have to climb stairs in order to move about your home or do laundry if you had a mobility problem? You may want to design the home so that there are no elevation changes between outdoor areas, such as a patio or garage, and the main living area. These changes will offer easier access into or out of the home for a person with a disability. Hallways of the home should be wide enough to accommodate the use of a wheelchair or walker, and rooms such as closets and bathrooms should be wide enough to allow a wheelchair to be turned around within them.

Mulit-level homes create problems for people with mobility issues

A ranch design is the most adaptable as you age. Even though a ranch design is more spread out, its single level makes mobility much easier than any other home design. Another option is the use of pocket doors instead of hinged

doors in key areas, such as bathrooms, toilet enclosures, or closets. In these limited space areas, hinged doors are difficult for an able bodied person to use, let alone a disabled person. Many new homeowners actually remove hinged doors from these areas, because they are so difficult to open and close. Pocket doors, on the other hand, can slide out of the way for easy access, while still offering privacy. These considerations can be designed into your home before construction begins. Moving walls, and changing doors, after the initial construction of the home is completed can be expensive. Counter heights can be another concern for disabled people. People in wheelchairs cannot easily use standard height counters in kitchens and baths, because they are too high, and do not have any legroom beneath them. Counters in kitchens and baths can be changed to accommodate life-style changes more easily moving than walls, and changing doors.

Build Within Your Budget

When considering the task of building a home, you need to consider the budget. The budget is the amount of money you can spend on a home while allowing for the other bills of everyday life, and for unexpected circumstances. The initial cost of the home, the interest on the home loan, municipal taxes, and insurance will determine the monthly expense of the home. Your banker or a mortgage company can determine the size of the home loan for which you qualify.

The quality of your interior finishes will greatly affect your building cost

How much home can you really afford? How many people do you know who have purchased more house than they can afford? They have a beautiful facade with no furnishings. This is commonly called "house poor". These people are constantly worried how they will pay their monthly bills, which causes stress, anxiety, and is in general, unhealthy. Money, or lack of money, is one of the leading causes of the breakdown of the family unit today. Another concern is the job market. With all of the mergers, and takeovers of large companies in recent times, your job situation can dramatically change in a short period of time. These changes can also cause cash flow problems.

Buying or building well within your means will give you advantages over your peers. By building smaller, your building costs will be reduced. With your building costs reduced, your payments will be lower, allowing you more money for investments, or the ability to pay off your home loan in a shorter period of time. You may also have more money with which to send your children to college, travel, or even be able to retire early. These lower expenses can also be valuable in times of financial stress, which most people

experience at some point during their lives. Many people experience this at several occasions during their lives. Owing less money every month may mean the difference between survival and bankruptcy. Keeping your expenses well within your current means has several advantages.

Do not borrow the maximum amount of money for which you qualify. Lenders use a mathematical formula to determine how much home for which you can qualify to purchase. This formula takes into account your history of debt payments, your current income, and your current debt load. These formulas are supposed to keep the lender, and the borrower safe from financial problems (overstretching your finances). Many times, this process does not work too well, because either the borrower is not completely truthful about their finances, or the lender is too eager to establish a new loan. In either case, the borrower can get into a position where they cannot effectively make their home payments, which causes financial stress. Keeping the cost of your home lower will normally prove the wiser choice.

Once you have determined a budget, you now must make some other choices. These choices involve the quantity and quality of space in your future home. Which of these is more important to you? Higher quality construction will increase your cost, where as a larger home (more quantity), will also increase your cost. You only have so much money to spend; you must decide how you will divide up your resources on these two options.

The balance between cost, quality, and quantity is easy to visualize. If you

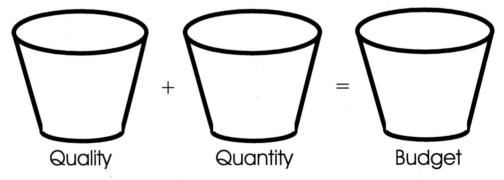

Quality + Quantity = Budget

Everyone has a budget when building a new home, it is important not to overspend

have three buckets: one labeled budget, one quality, and one quantity. Assume the size of all three buckets are the same, and the budget bucket is filled with sand, equal to your building budget (the sand is the money in your budget). You now have to decide at what ratio you want to add sand to the quality and quantity buckets, or at what ratio to invest in your future home. You can add more sand to the quantity bucket and less to the quality bucket. If you increase quantity, you have to sacrifice the quality of your home. You will not be able to have higher quality finishes, and materials such as hardwood floors. You will have to settle for less expensive options such as carpeting or vinyl flooring. Will this home feel comfortable to you? Will you be happy with what you have purchased, and be able to live with your choice for the next 10 years? Will the components used in the construction of your home last as long as you expect them to, or as long as they should?

You can choose to add more to the quality bucket than to the quantity bucket. If you increase quality, you will need to build a smaller, more efficient home. You will be able to finish the home in any style or texture you desire. There can be wood trim on windows and doors, as well as hardwood floors. You could also have the kitchen of your dreams. You however, may not be able to have other specialized rooms, such as a home office or sunroom. A more efficient floor plan compliments the choice of higher quality.

The balance between quality and quantity must fit your desires, needs, and budget. If you can eliminate wasted space, and have rooms serve double duty, you will have more of the budget available for quality, while still satisfying your quantity needs.

Build to Last

How long should a house last? How long will you stay in your current location? Can you recoup the investment of building a higher quality home if you do need to sell at some point in the future? Many homes today are not built with the building life span as a factor. Building a home to last longer costs more money, because of higher quality workmanship, and more expensive, longer lasting materials utilized in the construction. Most builders will not spend extra money on increasing building life span, because of the increased costs that can mean fewer home sales. Homes may be built to meet the local building codes, but this does not mean that there will not be foundation problems, water problems, or maintenance required shortly after construction is complete.

Masonry construction can last many years

Today, many homes are built with short-term materials used in key locations. Roofing materials can be of moderate quality, and may not be installed to manufacturer specifications, voiding the warranty. Exterior siding materials may only last only 20 years.

13

Composite wood siding is an example of such a short-lived product. This material is inexpensive, and an effective exterior siding material, but problems will occur if proper maintenance is not performed to prevent deterioration of the siding. If not well maintained, this type of siding can swell from water absorption, crack, bulge, and begin to fall apart. Composite wood siding is even used on expensive homes in order to save on construction costs. Better materials cost more money, and may require that some other features of the home be sacrificed in order to maintain the home budget.

Lack of mainte-
nance will shorten
the life of any
building material

What causes homes to have short lives? The two main culprits of building deterioration are water and sunshine. With all other things being equal,

material quality and workmanship, water is the most damaging element with sunshine being the second most damaging. Additional problems are caused by drastic temperature variations as the seasons change, or damage from insects.

Water, or moisture, causes most building materials to decay, rot, or fall apart. Designing a home to remove water from around a building will greatly increase its life span. How is this accomplished? You have to start from the ground up. A well-drained, and adequate foundation is the key element. Providing adequate drainage will help to keep the foundation from settling. If the foundation settles, stresses are placed on the entire structure, which can damage a building or create new points of entry for water into the structure, causing additional problems. Above ground, it is essential to use good quality building materials, and to design the home to eliminate or reduce the areas for water intrusion into the structure, in order to increase the life span of a building.

Sunshine is damaging to our skin, and to the skin covering most buildings. The intense heat, and ultra violet rays of the sun cause all paint materials to slowly fail. These paints will fail at different rates depending upon their chemical nature, quality, and application quality. Sunshine also damages, and destroys varnishes and stains. All of these coating materials are designed to protect the exterior sheathing materials of a building from the elements.

14

Once the paint fails, water is allowed to permeate the material, and sunshine is allowed to directly strike the finish material, both of these will shorten the life span of the finish material, and the building.

How long should a home last? A good target might be 150 years or longer. The potential increase in building cost depends on the construction materials, construction method, and craftsmanship used in the building. In some instances, the increase in building cost can be quite small. Building to last makes sense, not only on a personal level, but also on an environmental level.

Quality building practices and maintenance will improve longevity

Too many homes are built to last only 50 years. This is a terrible waste of our natural resources. Many of these resources are of finite supply or cannot be replaced in the near future. By wasting these resources, we limit the choices we will have in the future for ourselves, our children, and their children.

Can you recoup your investment if you do build to last? This depends mainly on how long you plan to live in your home. If you live in your home for 20 years, and your extra investment in long lasting materials was kept to a reasonable amount, you should be able to have a positive return on your investment in your home. This is possible because longer lasting materials will usually require considerably less maintenance than cheaper, shorter-lived materials. The less maintenance that you have to perform on your home, the less money you spend on a yearly basis for upkeep. These are called the "life cycle costs" of a material. Less expensive materials will generally require more frequent maintenance, reducing the benefit of the initial cost over time. More expensive materials will generally last longer, and require less maintenance, offsetting their higher initial cost over time. Exterior maintenance of your home can be expensive. How much does it cost to get a quality paint job on the exterior of a home? Call a local painter; you may be shocked at the price you are quoted. If you use better materials that do not need painting as often, and invested that amount into the construction of your home, you should end up on the winning side of the bargain. Again, this is only if you plan to live in your home for an extended period.

Don't be mistaken, when you sell your home, only a few buyers will consider the extra quality you have invested in your home. Also, most Realtors will not be very interested in listing your home if the selling price is higher than other homes in the area, regardless of quality. Most homes are sold using square footage, and the location as the general indicators of value.

Build to Preserve the Environment

We need to change our building practices so that they become more environmentally friendly. This is often called "sustainable architecture" or "building green". Improving upon existing building methods or utilizing alternative building methods such as insulated concrete forms, and utilizing alternative building materials can accomplish this goal. We need to build using resources, which are replaceable in our lifetimes. The areas where we can have the greatest impact are in the use of resource efficient building materials, and in the reduction of the waste created during the construction process. Much of the waste generated during the building process can be recycled into some useful form.

Reducing the waste generated during home construction is important to our environment

There are several alternatives in the area of resource efficient building materials. One option is to modify existing building methods so that they become more resource, and energy efficient. An example of this in wood framed homes is to utilize an advanced framing method. This reduces the quantity of wood used in construction, and increases the depth of the walls, allowing for additional insulation. Other examples involve alternative building materials, such as insulated concrete forms or straw bales. This subject is covered more thoroughly in chapter 4.

How much pollution and waste do our current building methods produce? If you examine the building methods used in most homes today, you would find excessive amounts of waste. This waste, for the most part, goes straight to our local landfills. The most common building method for residential homes today is with wood, and is called stick-framing. 95% of all homes built in the United States are stick-framed, and 10 to 15 percent of all the wood purchased for building these homes is discarded as waste. This waste consists of dimensional lumber cutoffs, plywood, and OSB (oriented strand board) pieces. This waste can be recycled in several different ways. It can be collected and shredded into mulch for use in gardening or public parks, used as fuel for various purposes, or used to manufacture additional products. Many building practices also utilize resources that cannot easily be replaced. An example of this is the harvesting of old growth forests to provide wood for new homes. Alternative building materials, which are more abundant, and more energy efficient, can be utilized to reduce this issue.

About 15 percent of all drywall purchased for construction is also discarded. Drywall waste is generally in the form of small pieces or odd shapes. This waste can also be recycled. Drywall is made mainly of gypsum, a natural mineral, with an alkaline base. If it is ground into a powder, it can be used in gardening or farming as a soil conditioner.

These are just two examples of construction waste, and possible uses for that waste, there are many more possible uses. With current construction methods, almost every part of the construction process creates some amount of waste. Could using different construction methods decrease this waste? Could we increase the amount of recycled material that is used in home construction? You may be able to find a contractor with a recycling program for their building waste. Some builders promote the use of waste construction material by local residents for what ever their needs might be (crafts, projects, etc.) Contractors often find they have a win-win situation when they recycle, because they

Straw bale homes are an example of sustainable architecture

are seen in a favorable way by environmentally conscious homebuyers, and the construction waste is put to good use. The builder also benefits from not having to pay to have as much waste material hauled to the local landfill. Some cities have developed programs with builders to help accomplish most of these goals. An example is the green builder program of Denver, Colorado. This program is designed to raise public awareness of environmental issues, and to use market pressures to change construction industry practices. This can be an effective method to implement change in the building industry. Builders who participate have an opportunity to attract more customers, and the city gets more efficient and environmentally friendly homes.

Build for Energy Efficiency

Can we improve the energy efficiency of our homes? How much will this cost? What are the advantages, and disadvantages of building energy efficient homes? Many of the construction methods used today are not very energy efficient. They are efficient from a construction efficiency standpoint, but they are inefficient in their ability to conserve resources and energy.

Fiberglass is the standard insulation material used in most homes

There are several ways to achieve better energy efficiency in a home. The most common improvement is to increase insulation in the exterior walls, roof, and floor. Increasing the insulation in a home slows the transfer of heat out of, or into the home, much the same as when you put on your coat on a winter day.

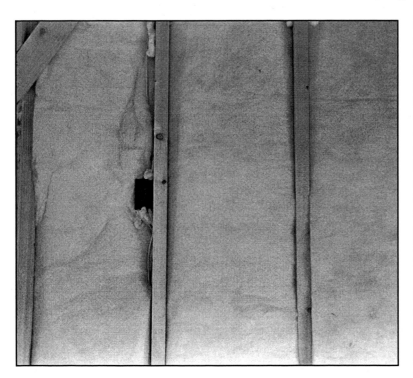

There are also alternative insulation materials available, some of which are more efficient than standard fiberglass insulation. Sealing the shell of the home with an air infiltration barrier to prevent air movement within, and through the walls will also increase energy efficiency. An air infiltration barrier reduces the amount of outside air infiltrating into the home, and reduces the heat loss, or heat gain associated with this process. A large portion of the heat energy in a home is lost through air infiltration.

Proper design can also increase energy efficiency. Placing windows on the south side of the building can help with solar heat gain in the winter, while designing the roof overhang to block direct sunlight in the summer reduces heat gain when you want it least. The type of windows used is also important in conserving energy, or allowing natural heat gain. Limiting the number of windows on the north side of your home will save energy. Designing the home with entry door air-locks will dramatically reduce air infiltration into the home, and improve energy efficiency. Designing your home to take advantage of natural cooling can also reduce energy usage. If you can eliminate the need to run your air conditioning for 2 additional months in a year, how much energy will you save? Using efficient mechanical systems (heating and cooling system, hot water heater, etc.) can also greatly improve energy efficiency. The largest portion of your utility bill is spent to power these mechanical systems. Additionally, you can reduce energy usage by purchasing more energy efficient appliances for your home. Lighting systems comprise only a small portion of a standard utility bill, but the use of energy efficient lighting fixtures can also help reduce energy costs. Compact fluorescent fixtures are about four times more efficient than standard incandescent bulbs.

There have been improvements in insulating materials and techniques in the past decade; however, the efficiency of the end result is still far below what is achievable. The R-value of the walls in most homes may not exceed R-15 at best. The R-value is calculated in the middle of a wall cavity where there is the most insulation, or the point in the wall with the highest insulation value. The R-value at a stud location within the wall may only be R-6. This means that about 15% (or more) of your wall has only an R-6 rating, and not an R-15 rating (R-values are explained in more depth in chapter 5). This does not take into account the air infiltration associated with stick-framed walls. These ratings are far below what is achievable with other building materials. These alternative building methods and materials may increase the initial cost of the home, but they will also increase energy efficiency of the home. Again, if you plan to live in the home for an extended period of time, you should more than recoup the additional construction costs, have a better home, and conserve natural resources.

Build a Healthy Home

Building practices today produce tighter, and more energy efficient homes than were constructed 20 or 30 years ago. A tighter home allows the indoor air to be exchanged less often, or fewer times per day than homes built in the past. More synthetic building materials are also being used in our homes. Many of these materials emit or off-gas or release chemicals into the home. All of these factors can combine to make the air inside a modern home polluted, and un-healthy. The U.S. Environmental Protection Agency reports that indoor air can be two to five times as polluted as the air outside the home. Most people, some much more than others, are effected by the chemicals off-gassed by building materials, by chemicals we use daily in our homes, and by things that grow and collect in our homes.

Many building materials

Wood flooring will not hide or trap indoor contaminates as opposed to other floor coverings

emit, off-gas, or release a variety of chemicals into the home. One of the most common chemicals released into the home is formaldehyde. Formaldehyde is a colorless, strong smelling gas, and is used in a variety of building materials, as a component of some adhesives. The most common sources of formaldehyde emissions in the home are cabinets, furniture, some types of plywood, and particleboard. Exposure to formaldehyde affects people in different ways, and to different degrees. For most of us, this chemical will have no noticeable effect, although the chemical smell may be strong. Some symptoms experienced by chemically sensitive people are watery eyes, irritated throat, nausea, skin rashes, headaches, dizziness, etc. Formaldehyde is just one example of an unsafe chemical present in most homes. There are other chemicals present in our homes, most of which are released by the occupants. Cooking, cleaning chemicals, pesticides, and paints are just some examples of products that can release volatile organic compounds (VOCs) into the atmosphere of a home. These chemicals can be irritating, and even harmful to our health.

Ceramic tile is another healthy flooring option

People spend about 90 percent of their time indoors (work or home). People who are the most susceptible to chemical exposure spend even more time indoors: small children, people with asthma, pregnant mothers, elderly, and people with illnesses. As new homes are built to be more energy efficient, built to allow less frequent exchanges of the air inside the home with the air outside, they also trap many of the chemicals we use in our homes. Children may be more susceptible to these chemicals than adults, and the effects can be life long.

Other things in our homes that may cause health problems are biological. These include microorganisms such as dust mites, plant allergens such as pollen, and molds or mildew. Many people are allergic to the feces of dust mites, which are present in every home. Specifically, dust mites live in our bedding, and feed on the dried skin that falls off of our bodies. Breathing these contaminants can cause allergic reactions in some people, and cause additional problems for people with asthma.

You can compromise and remove the largest sources of chemical emissions from your home without greatly increasing your building costs. The three areas where you can have the most impact on improving the air quality in your home are your choices in floor coverings, cabinetry, and the heating, ventilation, and air conditioning (HVAC) system.

The cabinets in your home are a source of formaldehyde. Most cabinetry uses hardwood plywood, most of which is manufactured with urea formaldehyde resins. These resins off-gas formaldehyde into the air of the home as they age. You can reduce the chemicals released into your home by selecting cabinetry constructed with hardwoods or plywood that do not use urea formaldehyde resins. The finish applied to the cabinets may also be a source of off-gassing solvents. Selecting clear, water based finishes will reduce this problem.

The flooring or floor coverings used in your home are another factor. Some flooring materials can emit volatile organic compounds (VOCs) into the home, while other flooring materials can trap unwanted contaminates inside the home. VOCs emitted by flooring materials can be a result of the materials used to make the flooring product, or the adhesives used to secure the product to the floor. Most carpeting emits VOCs.

A air-to-air heat recovery ventilator can help keep the air in your home fresher and healthier

Biological contamination is another source of irritation and illness associated with flooring materials, especially carpeting and area rugs. These products are a wonderful breeding ground for all sorts of contaminates. These contaminates can be dust mite dander, dirt, dust, hair, chemicals, etc. Breathing these organisms or contaminates is unhealthy. There is no way to keep things from growing or collecting in your carpeting, so the best choice may be to eliminate or limit the

Heat transferred to fresh air

Stale indoor air to be exhausted

Fresh outdoor air to come indoors

areas in your home where these contaminates can collect. Consider vinyl flooring, hardwood flooring, or ceramic tile as options. Hardwood or tile flooring is much easier to keep clean than any type of carpeting or area rug.

When we create more airtight homes, and we reduce the number of times in a given day that we allow the air to be exchanged, we create new problems. We trap in our homes the chemicals, dirt, dust, and biological contamination released or growing in our more efficient homes. We effectively create indoor air pollution. This, of course is also unhealthy. Now we have created the need

21

to remove contaminated, stale air from our homes without removing the conditioning of that air (heating or cooling). This is most effectively accomplished with an air-to-air heat recovery ventilator (HRV), which can be attached to your home HVAC system. The heat recovery ventilator removes stale, contaminated air from your home, and replaces it with clean air from the outdoors, while retaining 80% or more of the indoor air conditioning.

Another device that is helpful in maintaining good indoor air quality is an efficient filtration system on your HVAC system. The standard filter on most heating systems does very little to remove anything but large particles of dust, and lint from the air in your home. There are several different types of high performance filters available; electronic filters or media filters (a highly efficient paper filter) are examples. These more efficient filters are designed to remove more debris from the air that passes through them. These can also help to remove some of the irritating substances from your indoor air. High efficiency filters can be up to 30 times more effective than a standard furnace filter. If you do choose to have carpeting or rugs in your home, you can reduce the effects of the microorganisms and dust stirred up during vacuuming by utilizing an efficient HVAC filter. An efficient furnace filter can capture the debris stirred up as you vacuum your home if you run your HVAC system on fan only mode. This circulates the air in your home, drawing the particles into the filter system, and removing them from the air. Assuming you have a high efficiency filter system, this will give you cleaner air in your home, and potentially fewer health problems for your family.

A paper media filter can greatly improve the air quality in your home

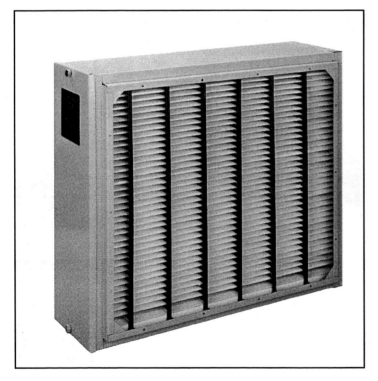

Vacuuming your home picks up things in your carpeting and on your flooring, throwing them into the air (most vacuum bags only capture the large particles). This debris, stirred up during vacuuming, can be irritating to some people. Another option that can be incorporated into your home is a whole house vacuum system. This type of vacuum system allows you to clean your flooring as with any other type of vacuum, but it has the advantage collecting all of the debris in a central location, while venting the exhaust to the outdoors. This greatly reduces the amount of contaminates (dust, dirt, dust mite dander, and allergens) being thrown into the air inside your home. Removing these contaminates to outside the home can have a healthy return for your family, especially if any family

22

members have allergies.

Radon gas is a health hazard for many homeowners. Radon is a naturally occurring radioactive gas, which is present in the ground and water in some parts of the United States. Radon is produced as Uranium (a natural radioactive mineral) breaks down, and is a leading cause of lung cancer in this country. Radon gas seeps into basements and living areas through small cracks in the foundation of the home. This allows the gas to collect in the living areas where the occupants breathe it. Complicating this problem, radon is colorless, odorless, and you cannot know if you will have a radon problem until after your home is constructed.

Precautions can be taken to eliminate the gas after the home is built. During the construction process of the basement or foundation, a relatively inexpensive piping system can be installed in the foundation of the home ($500 to $1000 extra cost). This piping cannot easily be installed after construction is completed. The system is not used until the home is finished, and can be tested for radon gas accumulation. If radon is found, a small electric blower motor is installed in the piping system to vent the gas harmlessly to the outdoors.

Radon gas in homes is considered a leading cause of lung cancer

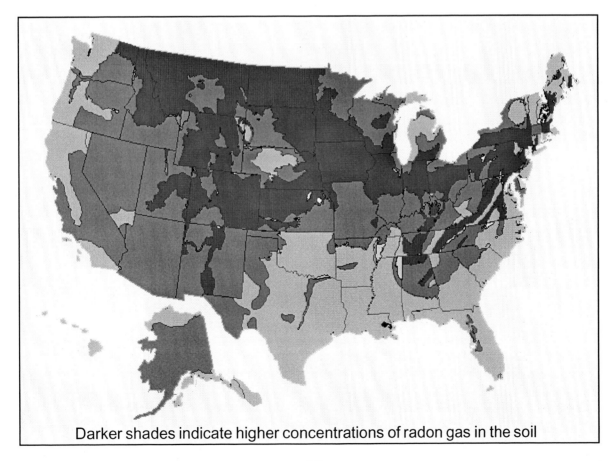

Darker shades indicate higher concentrations of radon gas in the soil

Another source of indoor air pollution comes from the chemicals we use in our homes on a daily basis. Take a look in the cabinet where you store your cleaning chemicals. Many of these chemicals are highly toxic when released into the air, and can be fatal if consumed internally. How healthy do you think it is for your family when you release these chemicals into the atmosphere of your home? One way to reduce these chemical emissions in your home is to use less toxic cleaning supplies. There are alternative-cleaning supplies available. There are also several books available, which reveal the nature of the chemicals you use today, and what the alternative products are. Switching to other cleaners may improve the health of your family.

Common cleaners are one source of indoor air pollution

Yet another substance in our homes that we consume every day is water. How clean is the water coming from the faucets in your home? Could this water be cleaner and healthier? Yes it can. Most municipally supplied water is considered healthy to consume, but may contain heavy metals (iron is common), fine debris, chemicals (e.g. chlorine, fluoride, etc.), and in some occasions, biological contaminates. These are all present after the municipality has treated the water. Water sources in rural areas will generally not be as clean, or may be nearly undrinkable. There are several mechanical systems available for cleaning and softening your water. Water softeners are common and effective, having the ability to remove most of the minerals in your water. Softening the water allows soaps to work better, making you, your clothes, and your dishes cleaner. Water filtration systems are also widely available and effective. These systems have the ability to filter out dirt, metals, and biological contaminates, or have the ability to produce very pure water by a reverse osmosis process. Cost and quantity of water produced are your only barriers.

Careful selection of building materials, furnishings, and chemicals used in a home can greatly affect the indoor air quality of the home, and thus influence the health of the occupants. Reducing the products that emit chemicals into your home can be accomplished by careful selection of the building materials. Building a healthy home will increase your construction costs, but this increased cost will be dependent upon the extent to which you address off-gassing and contamination issues. Normally, you will only increase your costs by only 3 to 5 percent. If extreme measures are required, your costs might increase 20 to 30 percent.

Build a Safe Home

Most homes are built to provide safety for the occupants. Depending on your location, extra measures may be needed to provide protection for your family from severe weather, or other circumstances.

There are several circumstances, which can threaten a home and its occupants, such as fire. Designing your home so that you have multiple access routes, or escape routes is a prudent measure. This is especially true if you have small children, or a person with reduced mobility living with you. In general, a single story ranch design will be easier to get into or out of than a multistory building. A multistory building can make escape or rescue much more difficult. If you decide upon a multiple story building, there are some measures, which can be taken to improve safety. Rope ladders in 2nd or 3rd story rooms can make escape possible in case of emergency. Designing the home with the roofs of lower rooms adjoining upstairs bedrooms can also provide optional escape routes. Daylight windows in basement living quarters are a good idea, and are required by most building codes. These provide an escape route from the basement if the stairs are not passable.

Smoke detectors should be included in multiple locations in every home. Multiple smoke detectors spread throughout your home will give your family the most warning in case of fire, and installing smoke detectors that connect to the electrical system of the home will increase their reliability (you never have to worry about replacing the batteries). You can also include a carbon monoxide (CO) detector in your home for added safety. Carbon monoxide is an invisible, silent killer, created by the burning of fossil fuels. Fossil fuels are gasoline, natural gas, propane, and other combustible materials like wood in your fireplace. If you have a leak in the flue for your furnace or fireplace, carbon monoxide can enter your home, make you sick or even kill you and your family. Combination smoke detectors, and carbon monoxide detectors are available to guard against both hazards.

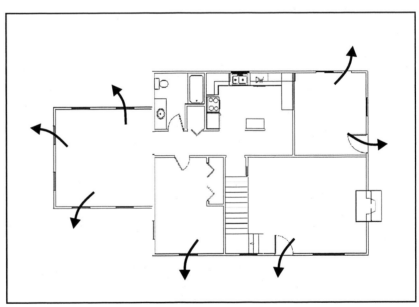

Multiple exit routes from a home are important in an emergency

25

A sprinkler system is another option for providing added safety to your home. Sprinklers are designed to protect your largest investment, your home. In some cases, they can also protect your family. Sprinkler systems are available with sprinkler heads (the fixture in the ceiling of each room that sprays water), which are unobtrusive. This allows the sprinkler system to be present, yet not detract from the aesthetic qualities of your home. Many insurance companies also offer discounts for homes with sprinkler systems.

Another aspect of safety is protection from intruders or burglars. One way to add additional protection for your family is a security system. Today, there are security systems available at a reasonable cost, and with a number of options. Most burglars will avoid a home with a security system, and move on to unprotected properties. Security systems are designed to monitor your home during the day, the night, or if you are not at home. This is done by the use of motion detectors, and contact switches on all doors and windows. Most security systems will also notify you if an exterior door is opened at any time. This allows you to know if a family member is exiting or entering the home, and also allows you to be aware of the presence of an intruder. You may then be able to evade and escape, or confront the individual. Security systems will normally include monitoring of smoke detectors, so if there is a fire, the alarm system automatically alerts the fire department. A security system may also increase the value of your home.

Another safety issue is the potential for severe weather experienced in several parts of the United States, which can destroy your home, or kill you and your family.

One example of severe weather is tornados, which are prevalent in the central United States, but can also occur in the south and southeast as well. Building an in-residence tornado shelter or safe room into your home is a very good idea if you live in these areas. A safe room is built from concrete, steel, or reinforced masonry, and should have a steel door. The room needs to be just large enough to hold all the members of your family for a short period of time. You should allow about 5 square feet for each person expected to seek shelter. Safe rooms are designed and built specifically to withstand the 300-mile per hour winds of the largest tornados, as well as flying objects carried by the winds at high speed. It is important that your safe room be located so that your family will have easy and quick access to its protection. Safe rooms can also offer protection from intruders. Your family can take shelter in the safe room, and wait for the intruders to leave, or for the police to arrive. These rooms can also be equipped with a telephone, or a panic button for the alarm system. You might want to add a safe room to your "Needs List".

In general, no home can be built to withstand a direct assault from a large tornado. Large tornados have winds in excess 300 miles per hour. You can have additional bracing added to help your home withstand the high winds of a near miss by a tornado. Virtually any building hit directly by a tornado will be completely destroyed. A basement will offer some protection from a tornado, however you should probably plan to build a safe room in your home for good measure. Surviving a tornado is your goal; your home can be replaced.

Flooding is a more difficult problem to overcome. Flooding will usually occur in river flood plains or coastal areas, and is caused by excess rainfall, or hurricanes, which can produce extremely heavy rainfall and very high tides. The only way to protect your home from inland flooding is to elevate the home well above the expected flood level. In recent times, many people have lost their homes to higher than expected flooding. You can build your home on stilts or on top of an earthen mound to keep it above the high water.

A safe room can protect your family from severe weather or intruders

If you live in an area where hurricanes are probable, there is virtually no way to protect your home. Hurricanes can have high winds, in excess of 200 miles per hour, and very high tides called a storm surge. The storm surge is the most deadly part of a hurricane. You can build a safe room in your home to protect you from the high winds of a hurricane, but you cannot reasonably build your home to withstand a 20 ft. storm surge (20 feet above normal high tide). The storm surge washes over the land, and washes the land out from under the buildings, or covers the buildings. A storm surge can also travel many miles inland causing severe flooding. The government expects half of all future hurricane related deaths to come from inland flooding. A storm of this severity may only happen in the area where you live, once in 50 or 100 years. The problem is that you do not know how bad a hurricane will be until it is upon you, and then it is too late to escape. You can build a safe room in your home, at or above ground level to protect your family from flooding, and you should allow about 10 square feet per person in the room. Be sure that you build your safe room above expected 100 year flood levels, drowning in your safe room would not be considered safe.

Earthquakes are an entirely different problem. An earthquake is caused when the tectonic plates of the earth slide past one another, causing the ground to shift and shake violently. When the ground shakes, so does your house. In earthquake prone areas, there are special building code requirements designed to prevent your home from falling in on top of you. The building codes will normally require heavy foundations with extensive steel reinforcement. Above ground, additional steel reinforcements are added to the structure to allow it to withstand the shaking of an earthquake. Again, surviving the earthquake is the goal; your home can be replaced.

You can find more information about safety, and safe rooms at the FEMA (Federal Emergency Management Agency) web site at www.fema.gov.

The items covered in this chapter are only general goals for your home. Each basic element has several sub-elements. Considering these issues as you design and build your home will help you achieve the end result you desire. Considering these things in the design and construction of your home will make it much safer, healthier, and more livable. In the back of this book, you will find a list of web sites containing information about manufacturers of products for your home. You can also find additional and updated material at www.futurehomestoday.com.

2   The Building Site

The first thing to consider when building a house is your building site or lot. The site will influence the type of home you build, the layout of the home, the access points, and just about everything else concerning your home. What type of land do you own or do you want to purchase? Flat prairie, wooded acreage, rolling hills, steep hillside, or a city lot are all possibilities. Is the land in the city, the country, or somewhere in between? Other considerations with any building lot are the condition of the land, accessibility to utilities, the proximity of the land to protected areas (wetlands for example), the foliage present on the lot, the views presented by the lot, etc. All of these will, and should influence the home you build.

The Land

You need to acquire your land, or at least know exactly where you will be building, before you begin to design your home. Why? You need to understand the characteristics of the land first because the location of the lot, the plants on the lot, and the surroundings will greatly influence the design of your home. A home is the combination of the land, and the house that it is placed upon.

"My prescription for a modern house: first, a good site. Pick one that has features making for character. Then build your house so that you may still look from where you stood upon all that charmed you and lose nothing of what you saw before the house was built, but see more."

--Frank Lloyd Wright

First, you will need some land to place your home upon

If you look around, you will see where people have not proceeded in this order. You will see examples where the style and placement of the home are contradictory to the surroundings and landscape. The home may look nice and be well kept; yet it will just not look or feel right. An example might be an alpine chalet on a barren city lot. The two (home style and lot type) do not work well together.

31

How can this problem be avoided? It can be avoided in one of two ways, you can buy a lot and design your home to suit the land, or you can have a home style in mind, and find a lot to accommodate that style. The first choice will provide you with the most flexibility, and will probably provide the most satisfactory end result.

Where should you start? You should probably start looking for land with a general idea of your needs in mind. These needs will identify the physical location of the property (a town or section of a town, within a specific school district, urban or rural area, a specific state, or even country). Once you have your general needs determined you can proceed to look for suitable land. With a little work, you will develop a short list of possible building sites. You do want to take your time and do your homework. The land is only the first part of a very large investment. You need to make a list of the individual characteristics of the various building sites, include the favorable and unfavorable features of each piece of land. Make a list similar to your home Needs List for this purpose.

Make a list of the desirable and undesirable things each lot has to offer

You and your spouse (if applicable) need to go to each lot, walk around and visualize the views you might have both from within your future home, and of the home from different locations on the land. You need to consider things like the neighborhood, local streets, various sources of noise, the existing foliage, etc. Add all of these to your list of good and bad characteristics for the specific lot. You may also want to take some pictures of the lot from various angles, attach these to your list once they are developed. Include price in your list. You may also want to visit the lots at various times during the day. You may have a situation where the local noise level is low during the middle of

Lot # 3 1634 S. Emery St.	
Good	Bad
Nice neighborhood Large trees Large lot Stream in back	Cost $45,000 Busy Street on EastSide Restrictive Covenant Ground water level ?

the day, but is too high in the mornings and evenings as people go to and from work. You may also want to consider changes to the land that you could make to correct existing problems, such as the view of an ugly neighboring building could be obscured by the addition of a group of evergreen trees or a fence. Pruning or removing some existing vegetation may also correct some problems. Yet another issue to consider is future development in the area. Too many people build homes in rural areas, only to have them overrun by development within 15 years. This development can obscure or remove some of the scenic views, and which might have been the reason for purchasing the land in the first place.

Once you have created your lists of various building sites, you should be able to narrow your decision down to the best one or two possibilities. You can then use your information to negotiate a price for the site of your future home.

Challenging Building Sites

What about unusual or challenging building sites? Challenging building sites are those where the land may have a steep grade, the soil of questionable stability on or adjacent to the site, or other issues that can make the lot difficult or expensive to build upon. These types of lots are available in most areas but extreme caution should be exercised before purchasing such a lot.

A challenging building site, if feasible to build upon, may offer spectacular and unobstructed views or other benefits of great appeal. These features, possibly including a low purchase price, are what give such a lot its appeal. You can design a home to work with, and accentuate these features, creating a special result.

Along with the desirable features, this type of lot may also have some undesirable features. These undesirable features are probably the reason why the land is still available for sale. The list of potential undesirable features is long and varied. These may be the physical makeup of the soil, the water level below ground, the grade or pitch of the land, proximity to protected land such as a wetland area, a neighboring road or building, etc. All or any of these will increase your building costs.

A steep or rocky building site increases construction problems and building costs

If you intend to purchase such a piece of land, you should strongly consider enlisting the services of a professional architect or building professional to help identify the barriers to building upon the lot, how to overcome those barriers, and the associated increased cost of building on the site.

33

Urban or Rural Land

Do you remember the theme song from the 60's television sit-com, "Green Acres"? Sorry, I know the song is now incessantly playing in your head but the words do have some meaning. Do you want to live in the quiet of the country or with the conveniences of the city? The city offers quick access to many places; you may have family who live in the city, or you may want your children to attend a specific school in the city. Some of the things that the city does not offer are, solitude, quiet, and some personal freedoms. A large plot of land may not be available in the city, if such a lot is available, the cost may be prohibitive or there may be restrictions associated with the building lot.

The City

The city offers quick access to stores and hospitals

Most of us are accustomed to the city. How long does a trip to and from the grocery store take, 30 minutes? What if the same trip took 2 hours? Close proximity to places may be one of the most important factors in your decision to live in the city. Take a few minutes and list the places you go during a week in a column, and how long you spend traveling to these places. Now, in an adjacent column, add an hour of travel time to each of those trips. Total up each column and think about the travel time involved, it becomes quickly apparent that you would have to become much more efficient in planning your trips for shopping or you might do without. Distances to friends and relatives may also be a consideration. Living in the country might isolate you from the people with whom you want to spend time. How long is your commute to work? What if you doubled or tripled your travel time for work, do you want to drive that distance every day, 5 days a week, 4 weeks a month, 12 months a year until you retire? You may

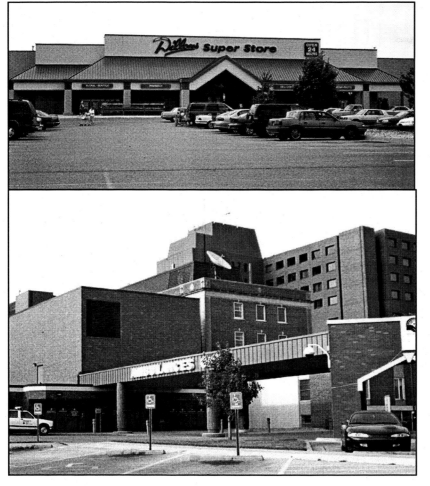

have to develop an affinity for books on tape to pass the extra time you would be spending in your car (many people on the east and west coasts make daily commutes of an hour or more, both to and from work). The city offers easy access to other places: hospitals, entertainment, schools, and stores are just a few examples. Would all of these factors change your view of living in the country after just a few months? Another issue could be the isolation of your children from playmates. Living in the country means your kids may no longer be able go across the street to the neighbors' house to play, again adding to your time spent in the car.

We also take for granted many other things which city life provides. How much is the clean water that comes from the city pipe worth to you? What if you had to have a pump, storage tank, a water softener, and a water purification system just to make your water drinkable? There are expenses associated with maintaining these items. What are the options for a sewer system? The two country options are a septic lateral field or a lagoon. A septic lateral field is the series of drainage pipes buried beneath the ground, and is used to disperse the treated fluids from the septic tank. If the land on which you live will not support a septic lateral field because it will not absorb the dispersed fluids, your option is a lagoon. A lagoon is a lovely open pond where the waste liquids from the septic tank are allowed to decompose and evaporate. Lagoons generally require little maintenance, but the family dog may decide to go for a swim in the lagoon before coming into the house (this is how inside dogs become permanent outside dogs).

Proximity to schools is important to many families

What about electrical power? Who is the last group of people to have power restored after a severe storm, the thousands of customers in the city or the few in the country? If you have ever lived in the country you know the answer. Another concern would be the lack of natural gas service in the country. The most common heating fuel option in the country is propane, which is more expensive than natural gas, and must be trucked to your location.

There are also disadvantages to living in the city. How often does the neighbor's dog or a loud car going down the street interrupt the quiet of the night? Man-made sounds are everywhere in the city. You may not notice them because of conditioning, but the sounds are there. There is a line from the "Blue Brothers" movie, "How often do the trains go by? So often you don't notice them." We get used to hearing sounds in the city, we just don't pay attention to them. You can go into your back yard on any evening and hear all kinds of sounds generated by people and vehicles. The noise from traffic next to a busy street can be loud and annoying. Visit your potential home site at several different times during the day, there may be much more noise during some periods of the day than at others.

Air pollution is a problem and a health hazard in many cities

Another problem with the city is our lack of solitude. Do you ever get tired of all the people who surround you in the city? Everywhere we go there are thousands of people. At the park, the grocery store, the cleaners, and at restaurants there are people. Many of these people may be rude, or they are in a hurry for unknown reasons. All of these factors add stress to our daily lives, which has a tendency to buildup and affect how we feel, how we treat other people, even those in our own families. Stress is generally unhealthy.

In many cities air quality is a concern. Air quality is affected by several sources. Industrial discharge and auto emissions are the largest contributors to urban air pollution. Many of our large cities have air quality warnings on a regular basis. How healthy do you think it is to breathe polluted air every minute of every day? There can be severe health risks associated with air pollution.

Crime can be another concern of city living. How secure do you feel about the safety of yourself and your family? Are there crimes committed in the area where you live or in an area through which you travel on a regular basis? Many cities have crime problems; these crimes vary from vandalism or burglary to murder. There are generally more serious/violent crimes committed in the city than in the country.

Other issues with city life involve personal freedoms. Usually, cities restrict what you can do in most areas. There are restrictions associated with some city subdivisions. These are generally in the form of a restrictive covenant, which is part of the documents attached to the purchase of a lot or home. These covenants can restrict where you park your boat or second car, or can restrict the types of materials with which you build and finish your home. If you choose to ignore these restrictions, and build your home outside these specifications, you may be forced to tear down what you have built and start over.

Yet another problem with living in the city is heat. Most cities are several degrees hotter (3 to 8 degrees) than a rural area. This is called the "urban heat island" effect. The city is hotter because of several reasons; there are more sources of heat in a city (houses, cars, industry), the roofs of most of these buildings are covered in dark materials, which absorb the suns heat, and much of the land in the city is covered in concrete or asphalt, and also absorb heat. All of these factors combine to raise the temperature in the city creating the urban heat island. This difference in temperature may seem like a small number but it can have a larger effect on your comfort level. This temperature difference also makes the mechanical systems of your home work harder, and use more energy in order to make you comfortable.

The Country

Country living can offer privacy and a quiet environment

Living in the country has some definite advantages and disadvantages, as opposed to living in the city. Have you ever been to a place in the country early in the morning when you cannot hear even a single man-made sound? If you haven't experienced this, maybe you should. One of the main advantages that country living has to offer is peace and quiet. The only noises you should hear on most days will be natural: birds, bugs, wind, animals, and so on are some of these sounds. Be aware that you might also hear a tractor, truck, airplane, or motorcycle, depending on your location and proximity to a road. In addition to the lack of man-made sounds, the country offers privacy. Privacy and the solitude that comes with it can be wonderful for the soul. Where do people from the city go on their vacations, to the

country for some peace and quiet?

Clean air is generally another advantage of country living. A home in the country is far from the pollution sources of the city: cars, airplanes, factories, and the chemicals they spew into the atmosphere are miles away. Clean, country air is healthier than the air in most cities. Odors are another consideration. Generally there will only be natural, non-disturbing odors in the country, but there can also be some bad odors associated with country living. There might be a hog or cattle farm 2 miles from your home. When the wind is blowing in the right direction, the odors from these farms can bring tears to your eyes. If you live next to a crop field, some of the chemicals used in modern farming can have irritating odors, and may be hazardous to breath. What about the road to a home in the country? In many parts of the country, rural roads may be dirt and gravel. In wet seasons, cars get covered with mud. In dry seasons, cars or trucks traveling the road stir up clouds of dust. If the home is situated next to the road, the house and everything around will be covered with dust. The next time you are in a parking lot, take a look at the cars. You will be able to tell who lives on a dirt road.

The country offers many personal freedoms such as having a pond

Previously discussed was the travel time associated with living in the country. This is a very important factor, and should not be ignored. Living in the country will also increase your travel time to the nearest hospital. This can be important in an emergency. Another issue is the potential for isolation in the event of severe weather. If there is a bad snowstorm, the country roads might be temporarily blocked or impassable. You could in effect be trapped in your home with no electrical power for several days. You might want to prepare for such possibilities by keeping some extra food on hand at all times, and consider purchasing a portable generator to power essential items like your furnace or refrigerator.

Living in the country does allow you many personal freedoms, which you would not have in any city. You can have huge garden or a large pond, or you could even build your own baseball field. You can paint your house pink, park your boat and camper in front of your home, and play loud music all night long (if your neighbors live some distance away). You can garden in the nude (also, if your neighbors live some distance away) or what ever strikes your fancy. Personal freedoms are one of the main advantages to country living.

Some other detriments to country living are the mechanical systems required for your home, which you will have to provide and maintain. These include a well for water, a septic system, and a lane or drive. All of these cost money to put in, and money to maintain. They also take time. Some or all of this cost can be offset by the fact that you will not have to pay a monthly water/sewage bill like city residents. City water and sewer bills can be $40 or more per month. The money saved can be spent on maintaining your country home mechanical systems. You will probably have more area on which you will want to plant turf grass, which means you will have to mow the grass, and you will have to invest in equipment to mow the grass. This equipment costs money, and requires maintenance. Mowing also takes time.

There are advantages and disadvantages to living in either the city or the country. You should be careful about your choices, especially if you plan on moving from one to the other, you might become disenchanted with the end result. Do your homework before moving from the city to the country or the country to the city, you want to make sure that you are making a decision with which you can live.

Orientation

Building your home with the correct orientation is probably as important as anything else you do in the building process. That is the orientation of the

Proper orientation of the home can help reduce your energy costs

house to the sun, not its orientation to roads or other buildings. The orientation of the house will determine how your home interacts with the sun, and may also determine the usefulness of some areas of your home as the seasons change. Proper orientation will also allow you to take advantage of the prevailing winds for cooling purposes.

In times before central heating and air conditioning, people built their homes to take advantage of the effects of natural heating and cooling. If you

look at the Spanish missions of the southwest, orientation was very important. These buildings were long and narrow. The buildings were positioned in an east-west orientation, with a long side of the building facing south. This south-facing wall allowed the sun to warm the building in the winter, the captured heat then slowly radiated into the living area. Small windows allowed light into the building but could be shuttered to hold in heat. In the summer, long porches provided cooling shade, while the windows and the orientation took advantage of breezes for cross ventilation. This arrangement made living in a hot, arid area easier.

The direction at which you will orient your home is important when you purchase a building lot. Orientation is important in areas with cold winters because it can help conserve heat, but it is equally important in hot areas as it can help you keep heat out of your home. It is very common for people to purchase a building lot, which offers a beautiful view: this can be a view of

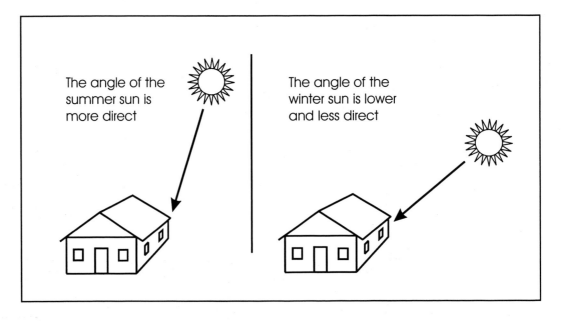

The angle of the summer sun is more direct

The angle of the winter sun is lower and less direct

The angle at which the sun strikes the earth changes from summer to winter

mountains, a lake, golf course, etc. People do not consider the livability issues of orientating their home toward a scenic view. You must also take into account how you will need to orient your home in order to take advantage of sunshine and cooling breezes.

In the summer in the United States, the sun at midday is at a more direct angle to the earth. When the sunshine is at a direct angle to the earth, less heat energy is reflected from the ground, and more energy is absorbed, this is why it is hotter in the summer. As the sun sets, the angle at which its rays strike the earth become less direct. If you have placed the windows of your home facing the west to take advantage of a scenic view, the suns rays will be focused directly into your home. The energy from the sun will enter your home, and

40

drive up the interior temperature, causing your air conditioning system to work much harder in order to keep these areas cool. Additional problems will be caused if you have a reflective surface between the sun and your home: a lake, pond, or a glazed tile patio will reflect additional sun rays into your living area, adding to the heat load your air conditioning system will have to deal with. In hot climates, you should consider it a general rule that you do not orient your main living/viewing area facing west.

If you have a porch or patio facing the west, the rays of the setting sun will also make this area quite hot, and potentially unusable until the sun has actually set. Even after the sun has set, the home and patio building materials will continue to radiate the heat energy, which they absorbed while the sun was shining. This radiation of absorbed heat may also make your patio uncomfortable. If you do have a patio, which receives too much afternoon sun, you may be able to improve the situation by adding a sun shading structure. This might be a roof over part of the patio, or the installation of a pergola. A pergola will normally have an open framed roof structure with lattice or a sunscreen material to block the sunshine. The main purpose of the pergola is to provide shade during times when you might be using your patio for entertaining or eating such as late afternoon or early evening.

A pergola can make the outdoor areas of your home more enjoyable

You also have to consider which side of your home will be the area where your family spends the most time, and which direction that side of the home should face. Generally, your home will have a public side, the entrance side, and a private side. The private side of your home will usually be the side that offers some seclusion from the rest of the world. The private side of your home may also face your back yard or patio. These two sides of your home will normally be opposite one another, but can be arranged differently to accommodate the lot location, desired orientation, and needs of the family. The private side will usually be where the common living areas are located. In areas with cold winter temperatures, the living area of the home should probably face south or southeast. This orientation will allow the sun to help warm both indoor spaces and outdoor or transitional living areas in the winter months. This

41

orientation will also allow the house to provide shade for a south facing patio in the early evenings.

You should visit your building lot at different times of the day. Take note of how the sun interacts with trees on the lot and other structures, which may be adjacent to the lot. This information may help as you start to visualize your future home, its layout, and how the sun will interact with the different rooms.

You may also want to engage a professional home designer or architect in the process of deciding the orientation of your home. These professionals will have experience with this issue, will most likely help you make the most of your location, and also help you avoid making a mistake in the orientation of your home.

Plants and Your Home

Shade from trees can reduce the amount of heat absorbed by your home in the summer

How important are plants to the livability of your home, possibly more important than you may initially think. Plants surround our homes and us. This is generally true in most suburban areas, more so in the country. Proper use of plants in conjunction with your home can have a positively effect on the comfort of your home, and can help to reduce your energy expenses.

If you purchase a building lot with existing trees, you should work diligently to design your home to fit within the existing plantscape. Trees, even small trees, add great value to a home. If you are not sure of the value of trees, go to a nursery to find out how much a 15' tree costs to purchase and have planted at your home, then you will have an idea of the value of a 50' or 75' tree. Keeping the existing trees on your land allows you to take advantage of the shade and beauty they provide. Trees also help to clean and cool the air surrounding your home. You can plant young trees in your landscape, but because trees grow slowly, the next owner of your home will most likely be the person able to take advantage of what your trees have to offer.

In most areas of the United States, plants change with the seasons. We can take advantage of the changes plants make as the seasons change, and a well-designed landscape can dramatically cut your winter and summer energy expenses. Effective landscaping can also reduce your water consumption, reduce your lawn maintenance, and help to reduce noise pollution. These benefits are in addition to the beauty plants provide.

In the summer when plants are in full bloom and full of leaves, the sun is at its highest angle, and the heat from the sun is very intense. We can use the shade of trees and vines to help cool our homes. Large deciduous trees provide large areas of shade. If these shade areas cover part of a roof or wall of your home, the sun is blocked and less heat is absorbed by the home. Less heat absorbed means less cooling is needed for the interior of the home. Vines or climbing plants can perform the same function. If these plants are allowed to climb a wall, the leaves will shade the wall from the rays of the sun, the shaded wall being cooler, transfers less heat to the interior of the home. Shading your home can reduce the indoor temperature by as much as 20 degrees Fahrenheit according to the U.S. Department of Energy, and a well planned landscape can reduce air conditioning costs by 15% to 50%.

Plants add beauty to any landscape

There are some precautions to take when integrating plants with your home. Trees near your home can have limbs break off and crash onto or through the house as they age or during severe weather, worse, the whole tree could topple onto your home. Vines attach themselves very securely to walls, some vines can cause damage to the wall structure or siding material. Providing a trellis, or lattice structure for vines to grown upon can save your siding.

Plants can be used in other ways to cool your home. Have you noticed how much cooler the air feels when you stand in a group of trees? The air is not only cooler because of the trees ability to block the sun. The trees use the energy from the sun to conduct photosynthesis, the process of which also releases large amounts of water vapor into the air. This water vapor can cool the surrounding air by as much as 10° F, as this cool air settles to the ground, it makes you feel more comfortable. If you have trees planted around your home, you can allow the cooler air beneath them to enter through windows and help cool your home. Vine type plants allowed to grow on a trellis over a patio can provide much needed shade, and also help to cool the air around your home.

Plants can also help to improve the efficiency of your air conditioning system. All air conditioning systems have a condenser unit located outside the home, usually beside the home at ground level. If this unit sits in direct sunlight, it is less efficient at dissipating the heat it generates while operating. By shading the unit, you can increase its efficiency by as much as 10%. This is just another example of how to save energy by using plants.

Tree rows can reduce winter wind speeds around the home, reducing energy usage

Plants that shade our homes in the summer may allow the sunshine to enter our homes in the winter. Deciduous trees (oak, maple, ash, hickory, etc.) loose their leaves in the fall. A tree with no leaves allows most of the sunshine and the suns heat energy to pass through its barren limbs, and into your home. This fact can be important if you plan to take advantage of passive solar heating with your home. It is important to note that some varieties of deciduous trees can block as much as 50% of the suns energy, even after loosing their leaves.

Trees on your property can also help conserve energy in the winter. In areas with cold windy winters, the wind can reduce the ability of your house to retain heat. People are affected by wind chill because the wind increases the rate at which we loose body heat. Wind has a similar but different effect on your home. As the wind blows past your home, escaping heat is transferred more quickly to the outdoor environment. Wind will also blow into and through any small spaces in your walls and ceilings, allowing cold air to enter your home and warm air to escape. If you can reduce the speed at which the wind passes over your home, you can reduce heat loss from your home, and reduce your energy consumption. A dense row of evergreen trees planted on the north and west sides of your home can reduce wind speeds around your home. The trees will block and slow down the wind in the general area of the home, the reduced wind speed helps to reduce the heat loss from your home. You can further reduce the wind speed around your home by planting a tree row on the east side of your home. Your heating costs can be reduced by as much 25% to 40% using this method as opposed to a home with no wind protection, this is why you see so many farmhouses with rows of these trees on the north and west sides of the property. For best results, plant the tree row a distance from the home equal to three to five times the height of the mature tree. This will provide you with the most effective windscreen. If you have heavy snows in the area in which you live, planting small shrubs on the windward side of your tree row will help to capture and trap the blowing snow, helping to reduce snow drifts against your home.

Plants can also provide privacy and sound absorption. Plants are often used to separate a home from streets and neighbors. A row of thick evergreens or shrubs can provide a dense screen, keeping people from seeing onto your property, or preventing people from entering your property. Plants can also be used to absorb unwanted sounds. Again, a dense row of evergreens or shrubs can help to absorb obtrusive sounds. This can be especially useful if you plan to live next to a busy street.

Yet another way of using plants can reduce your lawn maintenance, and your water usage. We in the US commonly plant more area than we need in lawn turf, which requires continual maintenance, and large amounts of water, and is not particularly efficient. Also, most lawns are cut with gas-powered lawn mowers, which do not have any pollution controls. According to the Environmental Protection Agency, a two-cycle gasoline lawn mower releases more carbon dioxide into the atmosphere in one hour than is released by driving a modern car several hundred miles. Many people also use chemicals to improve the state of their lawns. Runoff of these chemicals is a major source of pollution to ground water and local water tributaries. An option to lawn turf is to put some sections of your land into native grasses and flowers, allowing these to grow wild. These natural sections of your property will require no maintenance, and no water other than that provided by rainfall.

Design your home to best suit your building lot

These are only a few examples of utilizing foliage to make your home more comfortable. A hundred years ago, most of these methods, and several others, were employed by people whenever possible to increase their level of comfort. This was an era before air conditioning, insulation, or even effective heating systems. Effective use of plants can help

45

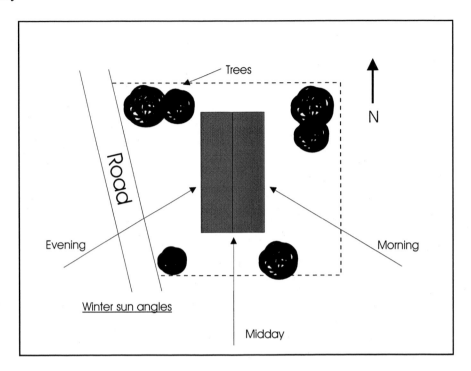

reduce your energy bills, and make your home more comfortable. Other advantages of plants around the home are the natural beauty they provide, and soothing affects they can have on people.

Placement of the Home

Now that you have acquired a building lot, and looked at orientation and foliage on your lot, you are ready to consider where to place your home upon your lot.

You need to visualize the placement of your home upon the lot. This is best accomplished with graphic or diagram. If you cannot draw, it is not a problem; the quality of the diagram is not a concern. It is the process of visually thinking through the placement of the home on the building site, and which should guide you toward the best compromise.

Start by making a rough sketch of the lot, the significant plants on the lot, and things that border the lot. These other things can be roads, neighboring houses, bodies of water, etc. You will want to make your drawing to a rough scale, such as 1/4 inch = 1 foot. Using graph paper will help you in this process. Draw the four points of a compass somewhere on your sketch, north, south, east, and west. Make sure that you orient your drawing with the orientation of the building site, north on the drawing with north on the site.

Now take some graph paper and cut out the general shape of your future home to scale. You can use the squares on the graph paper to estimate the size of the

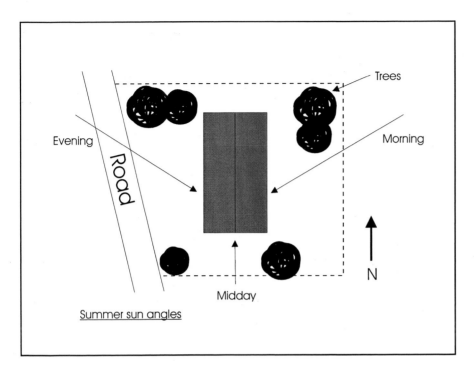

Trees

Evening

Road

Morning

Midday

N

Summer sun angles

home, again 1/4″ = 1′. Yes, you do not know how your home will be shaped at this point, but you are only trying to visualize how the home might, or could interact with the land and the elements. This process may give you some ideas to use once you do actually get to the design process.

Place the cutout of the home on the sketch of the lot. Try orienting the front of the home in different directions on the sketch. Look at how the home will work with the lot. Try to visualize the views from within the home. Think about how the sun will interact with the home, such as how the sun will shine in through windows at different times of the day. What rooms will receive sun in the morning, sun at midday, and sun in the evening? A home with a north-south orientation will not be able to efficiently take advantage of passive solar heating. How will the sun interact with your outdoor spaces? Will your patio have shade by late afternoon? Think about how your family will use the home, and how can you best utilize the land to provide privacy for your family? For each orientation, make a list of things you like, and don't like about this orientation. For the most favorable orientation, think of ways the home could be designed or arranged to take advantage of all building site has to offer, and which will make the best use of the building site. Try out different shapes of homes, looking for any that have advantages over others. Add these thoughts to your list, you can use it as you shop for home plans, or you can use it during discussions with your building designer or architect.

As you are doing all of this, you will also want to think about maximizing the usage of your land. As you know, the land you have purchased or are intending to purchase is very expensive. By maximizing the usage of your building

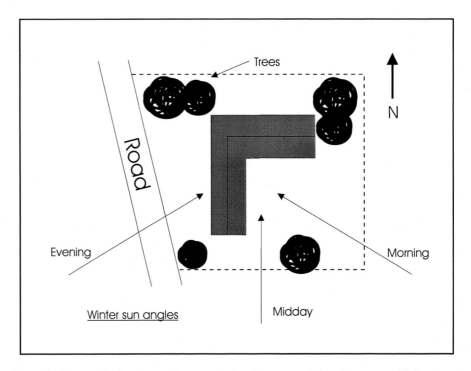

site, as in how you place your home on the site, you will make more efficient use of your land. You need to ignore what may be typical for placement of a home in the neighborhood, and think about how you can get the most from your land. You do however need to be aware of any zoning requirements for set backs (the distance you must maintain between the house and the street or other buildings), or any other restrictions associated with your building site.

With these restrictions in mind, look to see what happens if you build the home closer to the street than other homes in the area. It may be the case that the homes in your area are set back further from the street than is required by the law. If you can move your home closer to the street, you will end up with a larger back yard. What if you set the home at an angle to the street to take advantage of the sun (you do not have to build your home parallel with the street or other buildings)? What if you set the home at an angle, and moved it closer to the street? What if you build an "L" shaped house? These are only a few possibilities, there are many more. Play with different ideas, you may find something you like, and which has advantages over a more traditional placement.

Make sure you involve your spouse in these processes. You can guarantee that he/she will have different needs and ideas than you. Again, you will need to compromise to attain the best solution. You may also want to ask the opinion of relatives and friends. They may have some insight that you will find helpful. If you plan to use a home designer or architect to design your home, discuss all of the sketches and ideas with them. This will help to provide them with some insight into your needs and desires.

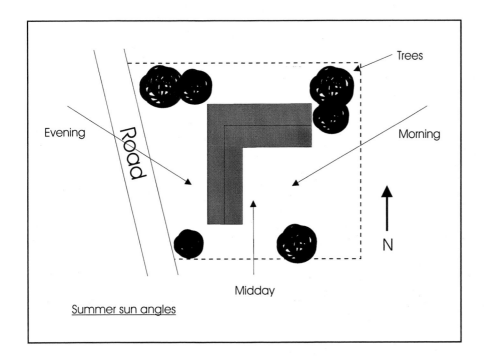

Trees

Evening

Road

Morning

N

Midday

Summer sun angles

As you can see, careful planning for your building site can greatly improve the livability of your home. Not only will you be happier with the completed combination, but you will also save energy, and reduce your maintenance costs. There are forms in Appendix A, in the back of the book, which you may find helpful as you consider your building site. These forms are also available in electronic version at www.futurehomestoday.com.

3   Building Materials

The earth has only a limited amount of resources. These resources may be renewable such as forests, or may be non-renewable such as minerals. These resources may seem limitless or may be very rare. People are the only beings of earth that deplete and destroy these resources as we make our lives. We consume, transform, use, discard, and pollute the resources of the earth.

Preserve and Conserve

You do not have to look any further than the trash we generate to see just how wasteful of a race we really are. Our trash says a lot about us. Most large cities have terrible problems finding enough space to dispose of trash generated by its citizens, partially because only a very small amount of the trash that people produce is recycled. Take a few minutes and look at what you throw out on a daily basis. Are there any recyclable plastics, aluminum cans, glass of any type, newspaper, or magazines? Most of these items can be easily recycled today; there is possibly a recycling station in your neighborhood for these items. We are able to discard these recyclable materials because they are cheap and plentiful, and it seems that it is not worth our time and effort to recycle these items today. This may be required in the near future.

A typical waste pile from a building site

If we look at the housing industry there is a considerable amount of waste in the construction process, most of which ends up in our landfills. Can we utilize more efficient building materials? Can we reduce the total amount of waste generated in the building process? How many recycled products are used in construction today? What materials are available as recycled or with recycled content? Are these materials cost effective? How much can we reduce our impact on the environment by using recycled materials? How does building longer lasting structures affect the environment?

By utilizing recycled materials, we can conserve our natural resources, reduce waste and pollution, and help to preserve our environment. By building homes that last longer, we can reduce the resources necessary for construction (labor and materials), and reduce the amount of debris that clog our disposal sites. By using materials that have less impact on the environment, we can

Concrete basement
walls and floor

Textured concret blocks
are used extensively in
commercial construction

help to preserve the environment for our children. By using materials that are more energy efficient, we can also reduce our impact on the environment. By doing all of these things, we will be using sustainable building practices. Building practices that will allow the construction of buildings, virtually indefinitely, because resources are utilized at a sustainable level.

Conventional Materials

In this section, we will look at how conventional building materials affect the environment. These materials consist of various types of wood, masonry, interior and exterior sheathing, and finishing products such as paints. Since these products comprise the bulk of the material used in the construction process, they also make up the bulk of the waste produced from home construction. The following section looks at environmental impact of common building materials, their longevity, and potential health effects of their use. These are only the possible effects of manufacture and use. Different manufactures will make the same product, and have different levels of environmental pollution; some of these pollutants can be controlled with proper handling while others are considered acceptable in our society. To totally eliminate all pollutants, we would have to discontinue the use of these materials, find alternative materials, or return to living in trees and caves. Being aware of a problem allows us to seek alternative materials and methods of manufacture, and construction that are less polluting.

Concrete

Concrete is used extensively in most homes built today, primarily in foundations, walls, and floors. Concrete is mostly used in its liquid state (as is comes out of the cement truck), and is poured on location to form a component of the house. Concrete is use in many other ways to manufacture products at remote locations, which are then shipped to the construction site. Examples are concrete shingles or tiles, concrete paving bricks, concrete blocks, and concrete siding. Concrete is manufactured from Portland cement (a mixture of limestone, clay, and sand) aggregates (gravel and sand) and water. There are environmental concerns from all phases of the concrete life cycle. The base components of concrete manufacture are mined or quarried. These mining activities can pollute surface water in surrounding areas with large amounts of sediment if not properly handled. There are emissions of huge amounts of carbon dioxide during the manufacture of cement, the binding agent in concrete that occurs during the heating process of the minerals,

Concrete is also used to make paving stones and retaining wall blocks

which make up the Portland cement. There is pollution created during the transportation of the components of concrete to the production site and the construction site, and lastly, there are huge amounts of concrete debris from building demolition, which end up in landfills. Once manufactured, concrete does form a very stable and strong substance for building construction with a projected life span of 100 years or more. Many ancient roman buildings and aqueducts are still standing because concrete was used as the mortar for setting the stones over two thousand years ago. Concrete emits little or no chemicals into a home once in place. Concrete also makes a good product for use as a thermal mass in passive or active solar homes. One method of improving the environmental friendliness of concrete is to substitute fly ash for a portion of the cement in the concrete mixture. Fly ash is a by-product of coal-fired power plants, and can replace as much as 35% of the cement in the concrete mixture. It adds strength and durability to the concrete, while consuming an industrial waste product. Concrete debris can be recycled, and used as solid fill material in various construction projects.

Brick

Bricks are manufactured by combining raw materials, clay, sand, and binders, into a form that is then fired (or baked) to harden them. Brick manufacturing has the potential to pollute the environment. The base components are quarried, and have the potential of polluting local waterways with sediment.

Once the raw materials are recovered from the earth, they must be processed, which requires energy and heat, much like cement manufacture. Again there are large amounts of carbon dioxide released into the atmosphere during the firing process. Once brick is manufactured, mortar is used as a bonding agent is needed to hold the bricks to one another. Mortar is basically cement with lime added to increase expansion characteristics. Mortar has the same pollution potential as cement. Today, brick is used as a surfacing product or veneer in many homes. Brick provides a very long lasting

Brick is used as an exterior surface on residential and commercial buildings

and stable surface, and should last as long or longer than the structural element of the house. One advantage of brick is that it requires very little maintenance as it ages. Demolition and disposal of brick structures is much the same as concrete structures. Brick does have the advantage of being more recyclable than concrete, as bricks can be cleaned of any mortar residue after a building is demolished. Used bricks are available from many sources but can cost almost as much as new bricks. It should be pointed out that a very large proportion of used brick debris is sent to landfills as waste.

Stone makes a beautiful, long lasting exterior surface material

Stone/Cultured Stone

Stone or cultured stone are other options for an exterior masonry finish on your home. Natural stone is quarried, and in general are very stable, although some soft stones will deteriorate relatively quickly when exposed to the elements. There are many different types of natural stone, limestone, granite, marble, and sandstone are very common types, but availability will vary through out the country. Most people will choose a type of stone found locally because stone is very heavy, and therefore very expensive to transport long distances. There is the potential for pollution of local waterways with sediment when the stone is quarried. Stone is almost always bonded together using mortar. Cultured stone is stone manufactured from concrete to resemble natural stone, and has the same pollution potential as any concrete product. Cultured stone is very popular in most parts of the country, and has one advantage over natural stone, it is lighter weight, and can be manufactured to specific shapes and sizes. Cultured stone can be bonded to a frame or masonry wall to give the appearance of natural stone at less cost, where as natural stone is very heavy, and requires a masonry foundation for support. Once manufactured and installed, both of these products will have a very long life span with minimal maintenance. Stone or cultured stone may be used inside the home, but neither they nor standard mortar pose any health threat to the occupants.

Dimensional Lumber

Dimensional lumber is one of the most common materials used in housing construction today, with 95% of all homes built use it as the main structural component. Dimensional lumber is made at sawmills from trees; spruce, pine, and fir (SPF) trees from the northwest make up the largest portion of the wood used in standard lumber. This wood is the white lumber we see used in home construction, SPF being used mainly for the vertical wall studs and horizontal plates of a stick-framed home. Hem fir or southern yellow pine are generally used for the flooring members and roofing trusses, as these woods are heavier, stronger, and better able to support larger loads. Southern yellow pine may also be chemically treated to resist decay. This lumber is called pressure treated (PT) or CCA lumber, and is the green lumber we see used

95% of all old growth timber in the United States has been harvested

in decks and some fences. The chemical used to treat this wood is a pesticide mixture containing chromated copper arsenate, which is forced into the wood in huge, pressurized tanks. Other special types of lumber such as cedar and redwood are widely used for exterior purposes such as siding, fencing, or decking. The manufacture of lumber presents several pollution concerns. There are problems with erosion when large numbers of trees are removed from a given area (common with clear cutting of large sections of forest); the soil on hillside is disturbed, causing huge amounts of dirt and debris to be washed away during rainy periods. This debris washes into streams and lakes, clogging them with sediment, and killing wildlife. Lumber companies

55

replant most forests as they are harvested, and is done to help reduce erosion, and to ensure a future source of lumber. There are pollutants released from transportation and manufacture of lumber. Roads are cut deep into the forests to allow transportation of the trees, making these roads creates additional erosion problems, and the trucks used to haul out the trees aggravate the erosion problems. Once the trees reach the sawmill, they are cut to the desired dimensions, and normally dried in a kiln. A

Dimensional lumber stack at a construction site

kiln is a large oven, which is used to reduce the water content in the lumber, reducing its tendency to warp. After the lumber is manufactured, it must be transported to the point of sale, which is accomplished with trucks, trains, ships, or a combination of the three. This manufacturing process and transportation of the lumber utilizes fossil fuels for power, and releases more pollutants into the atmosphere. These are unfortunately some of the consequences associated with lumber manufacture. Once lumber reaches a building site, the vast majority is used for construction of the home with about 15% being discarded as scrap. Most of this waste wood ends up in landfills. This does not have to be the case because this wood waste can be reused in several ways such as fuel, shredded and manufactured into other products, or shredded into mulch, and used by local residents. Some contractors now promote and work to reuse construction waste. There some potential health concerns

Dimensional lumber is used to build the frames of most homes

with CCA lumber, and the Environmental Protection Agency is concerned about the possible effects of these chemicals on pregnant mothers and their children. These chemicals also slowly leach out of the wood, and into the ground over several years. It is not recommended that this material be sawn indoors without the use of a particulate filtering mask, as inhalation of the sawdust should also be avoided. Recycling of CCA lumber should be done with caution. There is lumber available that comes from forests certified for using sustainable forestry practices. This lumber is available in most cities, but will cost more than lumber from non-certified forests. Some lumber supply companies have opted to carry only certified lumber. It should also be noted that lumber is a wonderful building material for many purposes. Roofing trusses, flooring joists, or anywhere that wood is used as an interior finish material are examples, but we can reduce the amount of lumber used as the main structural element of homes, and substitute other building materials.

Plywood

There are two types of plywood manufactured currently, softwood plywood being the most common. This is used for exterior sheathing, roofing, and siding in some new home construction. Softwood plywood is manufactured from soft lumber such as SPF using phenol formaldehyde resins as the adhesive, and will off-gas very little formaldehyde as the plywood ages. The other option is hardwood plywood, and is used mainly in cabinetry and paneling. Hardwood plywood is manufactured using urea formaldehyde resins, and does off-gas formaldehyde as it ages (the nasty smell you have with new cabinets). Softwood plywood does not pose much of a health hazard since the chemical emissions are very low, and this product is used primarily on the

Plywood (left) and OSB (right)

exterior of the home. Hardwood plywood can pose a health hazard as it does emit hazardous formaldehyde for a year or more, and is used mainly in the living areas of the home. Like most construction materials, there is a certain amount of pollution involved in plywood manufacture. Plywood has all of the pollution potential of any wood product, since it must be removed from the forest, and transported to the manufacturing site. The manufacture of all plywood also consumes fossil fuels, and involves chemical

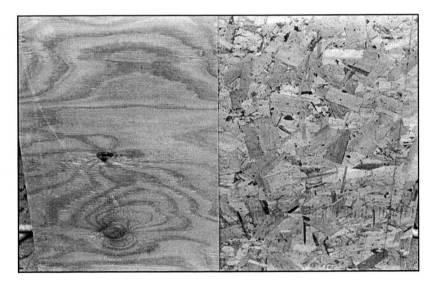

adhesives. Waste generated during plywood manufacture can be burned as fuel, chipped and used to manufacture other products, or shredded into mulch. Since plywood is not used as a primary structural element, other materials will normally dictate its life span.

Oriented strand board has replaced plywood for many constrution uses

OSB

OSB (oriented strand board) is a very popular option to soft plywood in home construction, and OSB has a couple of distinct advantages over standard plywood. The first advantage is cost, with OSB being considerably less expensive than plywood (30% less). For this reason OSB has basically replaced plywood, and is used as an exterior sheathing material on the walls, roofs, and some floors in homes. Another advantage is that OSB does not use wood from old growth forests for its manufacture. OSB is made from fast growing trees, which are harvested and shredded into strands or chips. These chips are then aligned in layers, pressed together, and bonded utilizing phenol based adhesive that does not off-gas substantial amounts of formaldehyde. The manufacture of OSB does involve all of the same aspects of soft plywood, and has the same pollution potential, less the destruction of old growth forests. OSB is also not used as a primary structural element; other building materials dictate its life span.

Particle board is a common compontent in cabinetry

Particleboard

Particleboard is made from sawmill sawdust or lumber reduced to sawdust. The sawdust is bound together with an adhesive. Most particleboard is bonded with urea formaldehyde (UF) adhesives, which can off-gas formaldehyde emissions into the home. Emissions of UF from particleboard are far lower today than 10 years ago. Also available, in lesser quantities, is phenol formaldehyde resin bonded particleboard that does not off-gas nearly as much as the more common particleboard. There is some pollutant release involved in particleboard manufacture, and includes carbon dioxide, chemical fumes, and particulate emissions. The manufacturing plant usually consumes waste from particleboard manufacture as fuel, and also releases pollutants into the atmosphere. Particleboard will generally last as long as the structure it is applied to if kept dry.

There are several forms of particleboard or similar materials, which have the same basic manufacturing process. These materials include hardboard siding and MDF board. MDF or Medium Density Fiberboard is a product that consists of a particleboard type material with a very smooth finish on one side. MDF has many interior and exterior uses, as it can be machined into many shapes, and accepts paint very well. This product is being used more and more as the interior trim in homes. MDF is also made using urea formaldehyde resins like most particleboard. To reduce the off-gassing problem, some manufactures are treating this material with ammonia during manufacture, which neutralizes the formaldehyde, reducing potential health problems, and the nasty smell. Some manufactures do offer MDF made without formaldehyde resins; however, this does make the product more expensive. MDF has a life span similar to particleboard.

Asphalt Shingles

Asphalt shingles are used on about 80 percent of houses in the U.S.A. Asphalt shingles are manufactured using a substrate of an organic material (wood chips and paper) or fiberglass. The substrate is the material that forms the shape of the shingle, and holds it together. Organic felt shingles hold up better in windy areas, while fiberglass shingles fare better in hot climates. Aggregate (substance that looks like small colored rocks) is bonded to the substrate using petroleum-based asphalt. Shingles are normally attached to the roof sheathing using nails or staples. Environmental issues concerning the manufacture of asphalt shingles focus on the petroleum bonding material and the manufacturing process. This process requires large amounts of fossil fuels, and releases heat and carbon dioxide into the atmosphere. Asphalt shingles will last 15 to 20 years in most climates, with some manufacturers warranting their products for 25, 30 or even 40 years, but these warranties only apply if the roofing product is applied per the manufacturers recommendations. There are also asphalt shingles that are designed to look like cedar shake shingles or even imitate the look of a slate roof; these shingles cost more than the standard asphalt shingles, but cost much less than the shakes or slate roofing.

Asphalt shingles

Cedar shingle roof

Wood Shingles

Wood shingles or shakes have been used as a roofing material for a very long time. In the past, wood shingles were one of the few effective roofing materials available. Wood shingles come in split or sawn form, and are made from cedar, redwood, or southern yellow pine, cedar being the most common. This product is twice as expensive as asphalt shingles, and will last 10 to 30 years in most climates. Wood shingles are naturally very flammable, and must be treated with a fire retardant in order to meet fire codes in many areas. Wood shingles cannot be used in some fire-prone areas of the country, because local building codes do not permit their use. The manufacture of wood roofing materials has the same pollution potential and environmental impact of any wood based product, and requires the harvest of old growth forests. This product does produce an attractive roof, however, there are better roofing materials available today. Wood shingles may also be used as a siding material for a home.

Composite Wood Siding

Composite wood siding is very similar in manufacture to particleboard, as it is manufactured from the same basic materials but with a finish texture. There is little risk of polluting the interior of your home with this product (off-gassing) since it is not used on the interior of the home. Pollution concerns are the same as with particleboard. Composite wood siding can cause other types pollution from the materials and labor required for maintenance since this siding

Composite wood siding

requires more maintenance than other siding materials. The maintenance interval for this product depends on the siding quality, paint quality, climate, sun exposure, and application quality. Repainting requires labor and materials. If not painted, this type of siding material can deteriorate, buckle, or crack, which requires replacement, needing more labor and materials. Composite wood siding will last 20 to 40 years if properly cared for, much less if not.

Vinyl Siding

Vinyl siding is an exterior siding product manufactured from petroleum based compounds. Vinyl is widely used on many types of housing today, because it is relatively inexpensive, and never needs painting. Vinyl siding also resists being dented by errant baseballs or small hail, but vinyl can crack if struck when cold. Environmental issues regarding vinyl siding focus on the petroleum compounds used to manufacture the product. Quality vinyl siding will last about 20 to 40 years, and requires only cleaning as maintenance during this period. There is currently no recycling program for discarded vinyl siding; it always ends up in the local landfill once removed from a house.

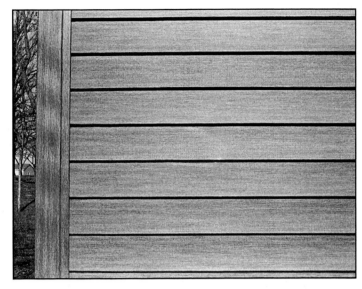

Vinyl siding

Aluminum Siding

Aluminum siding is constructed from a thin aluminum sheet formed over a substrate; the aluminum forms the exterior finish, and the substrate provides strength for the siding. Aluminum siding is coated with a long lasting paint finish. Aluminum is refined from bauxite, which comes from huge open pit mines. The manufacture of aluminum has the potential to create pollution during the mining and smelting process, and from the transportation of the raw and refined products. There are also vast amounts of energy consumed in the manufacturing process. Once the metal has been refined, aluminum is a very recyclable product, but aluminum siding however is rarely recycled. Because the aluminum is bonded to a wood substrate, any waste will normally end up in a landfill. As for longevity, aluminum siding will last 20 years or more if the paint surface lasts that long. Aluminum siding can be painted after many years on a house, but the finish quality never matches that applied by the factory. Aluminum siding is also vulnerable to denting, which may lead to early replacement.

Aluminum siding

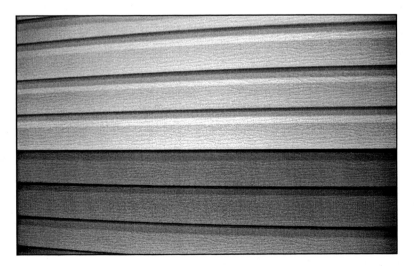

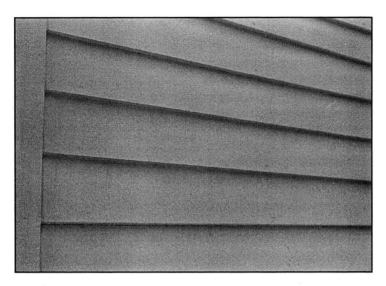

Wood clapboard
siding

Wood Clapboard Siding

Wood clapboard siding has been in use for centuries, and there are several types available. Wood siding is typically made from pine, redwood, or cedar, and can last for two centuries or more if properly maintained. Clapboard siding requires more maintenance, such as painting or staining to prevent deterioration, than do other siding products. Most wood clapboard siding will not last as long as it should, because people fail to properly maintain the product. Some trees used in wood siding manufacture cannot be replaced during the lifetimes of our children or their children. Because wood clapboard siding is a very expensive option, composite wood siding is much more widely used on modern homes.

Stucco

Stucco exterior
finish

Stucco is a cement-based finish material with an added pigment. It is applied to the exterior of the building in the form of a thick paste over a wire grid base. Stucco forms a very rigid shell on the building, and may develop hairline cracks over time, which require patching. These cracks can allow water intrusion, which can cause the stucco to deteriorate. There have been recent advancements in stucco technology that can eliminate some of these cracking

problems. This is typically called EIFS (Exterior Insulated Finish System), and uses a modified stucco coating applied on a foam insulation board. It should be noted that there have been some water damage problems associated with EIFS, and it may not be allowed in some cities. Due caution should be exercised, and a qualified contractor is strongly recommended with any stucco application. Stucco is mainly a cement-based product, and poses the same environmental risks as any cement product. A well-applied stucco finish can last 50 to 100 years with maintenance.

Gypsum Wallboard

Gypsum wallboard or sheet rock is used in most homes today, and is used to create a smooth surface on interior walls. The minerals used in wallboard manufacture are gypsum, limestone, clay, talc, mica, and perlite, all of these materials are natural, and in abundant supply. These products are mined, and can pose a pollution threat to local waterways. Gypsum wallboard is covered on both sides with a heavy layer of paper, most of which comes from recycled stock, which saves approximately 30% of the energy

Gypsum wallboard

required to make new paper (as well as a lot of trees). There are large amounts of water used in wallboard manufacture. This water can also pose a pollution threat if not properly handled. Wallboard itself produces little or no volatile organic compounds (VOCs) emissions but VOCs can be emitted from some wallboard joint compounds. Large amounts of wallboard are discarded during the construction process. This construction waste can be recycled by grinding the material up, and giving or selling it to farmers/gardeners for use as a soil amendment. Most builders do not take advantage of this property; they simply send their waste to the landfill. Gypsum wallboard will generally last as long as the main structure of the home.

Casement windows

Glass

Glass is used in many ways in home construction, but is used mainly as windows. Fiberglass insulation is made of the same basic material as windows, except in a very thin fiber form. Glass is made of glass sand, limestone, and soda ash, all of which are available in vast amounts. There is the potential for soil erosion and sedimentation of local water systems during the mining process, and particulate emissions associated with the manufacture of glass. Melting the raw materials also consumes fossil fuels, and releases pollutants into the atmosphere. Glass products, old windows, beverage containers, etc. can be recycled, however, most glass products end up as trash in our landfills. Glass poses no health treat from chemical emissions after manufacture.

Windows combine glass with a frame structure, which can be made of a variety of materials: aluminum, vinyl, wood, wood fiber material, or a combination of these. All of these materials have their own environmental risks.

Carpeting

Americans have become accustomed to the look and feel of carpeting in their homes. There are several issues regarding the manufacture of carpeting. Its manufacture consumes huge amounts of water, about 15 gallons is used to manufacture each square yard. Much of this water is not recycled, and is

Carpeting

reintroduced into the environment with little or no treatment. This water may contain manufacturing waste products that can threaten wild life, such as carpet dyes. Most styrene butadiene resin plants (a common component of carpet backing) also emit toxic pollutants into the air, creating a health hazard for surrounding communities. Carpeting and carpet pad emit low amounts of VOCs into the air of a home, while some carpet adhesives emit large amounts of VOCs. There are low VOC emitting adhesives available, and this is an important issue to people who are sensitive to certain chemicals. There are carpets available with non-styrene butadiene backing such as polyurethane. Carpeting manufacturers are moving toward more products with lower VOC emissions, and there are even some carpets available, which are manufactured from recycled soft drink bottles. Today, most discarded carpet ends up in our landfills. There is a plant under construction for the recycling of nylon-based carpeting. Carpeting will normally last 5 to 8 years in a home.

Ceramic Tile

Ceramic tile is a long lasting, beautiful flooring material, and is made from sand, clay, a bonding agent, and possibly a glazing compound. These materials are quarried, and have the same pollution potential as similar products. Ceramic tile is manufactured in a kiln, or high temperature oven, requiring the use of large amounts of energy, and releases carbon dioxide into the atmosphere (similar to brick manufacture). Once produced, ceramic tile is very stable, and releases virtually no chemicals into the home. Tile does need to be bonded to a surface with an adhesive such as mastic adhesive or thin-set mortar. Mastics are chemical based adhesives that contain a solvent, which can off-gas into the home. The mortar-based thin-sets do not generally off-gas any VOCs, but you may want to check the label prior to use. Ceramic tile should last the life of the home with minimal maintenance if properly installed. Ceramic tile is an excellent material, and has many uses in the home including floors, walls, and counter tops.

Hardwood Flooring

There are many types of hardwood flooring available. Traditional hardwood flooring is made from oak, maple, cherry, or southern yellow pine, and comes in various widths. This flooring typically has tongue and grove joints, and is about 3/4" thick. In the past, hardwood flooring

Ceramic tile

was finished with solvent-based materials, but there are water-based finishes available today. This type of flooring may require refinishing every 5 or 10 years, but can be sanded and refinished several times. Standard hardwood flooring will last as long as the home. There are other forms of hardwood flooring available today called hardwood laminates. This flooring uses a thin layer of the hardwood finish material, 1/8", which is laminated to more common, less expensive woods. This type of flooring is about 1/2" thick, comes pre-finished, and is glued or snaps together. Hardwood laminate flooring is usually installed as a floating floor, not being attached to the floor it covers. This material does provide a quality floor, but you may not be able to refinish it as with standard hardwood flooring. You can expect hardwood laminate flooring to last 7 to 15 years.

Hardwood flooring

Vinyl Tile and Flooring

Vinyl flooring comes in the form of individual tiles (1 ft. square) or as a large sheet of material. Vinyl is manufactured from petroleum products, and has the same environmental issues as other petroleum based products. Vinyl does off-gas some chemicals as it ages, most immediately after installation, and at gradually diminishing levels thereafter.

These chemicals are unnoticeable to most people but may be irritating to chemically sensitive people. Individual vinyl tiles usually come with a self-adhesive backing or must be applied with an adhesive. There is potential for the adhesive backing to off-gas irritating chemicals also. Vinyl sheet goods are applied to the floor by the use of mastic adhesive, which may have a potential for chemical off-gassing. Most mastics are solvent based, and emit VOCs. Vinyl flooring is not an espe-

Vinyl flooring

cially long lasting product, and it will last about 10 years before needing replacement.

Paint and Stain

Paints and stains are mostly produced from petroleum-derived substances, and are highly regulated due to the waste by-products produced. Paints, both organic solvent based and water based, can emit irritating chemicals or VOCs into a home, but there are paints available with low VOC emissions. Paints and stains are used on both the interior and exterior of homes to protect sheathing materials, and add color to the home. Paint or stain used on the

Paints and stains

exterior of the home will deteriorate, and be washed away by rain, releasing the chemicals in the paint into the environment. Care must be taken when disposing of any leftover paint or stain. Containers of these materials should be left open to dry up before sending them to the landfill or should be taken to a hazardous waste disposal site in liquid form. Liquid paint or stain should never be sent to a landfill or poured onto the ground as they can soak into the ground, and contaminate ground water.

Fiberglass Insulation

Fiberglass insulation is the most common form of insulation used in residential housing. This insulation is most common in two forms, batts or paper backed rolls. Batt insulation is manufactured to fit snugly in a wall cavity, friction holding it in place while paper-backed rolls are held in place by stapling the paper backing to the wall studs. Fiberglass insulation is generally manufactured using glass fibers, a bonding agent, and a paper backing where appli-

Fiberglass insulation

cable. Manufacture of this product, like most others, does produce some pollution in the form of carbon dioxide and particulate emissions. There is also the potential to pollute local waterways during the mining process of the raw materials. There is little or no health hazard associated from off-gassing of chemicals from fiberglass insulation, but the bonding agent used to attach the glass fibers to the backing may emit VOCs. There are health concerns associated with inhaling airborne glass fibers. Respiratory filters should be used during installation of the insulation, and until the insulation is sealed over with a vapor barrier and/or wallboard. Fiberglass insulation will last as long as the home.

Foam Insulation

There are several types of foams used in housing insulation today, the most common types being EPS (Expanded Polystyrene), polyisocyanate, and polyicynene. Foam insulation is generally made from petroleum based compounds, and a chemical that causes them to expand. Like any other petroleum-based material, there is a potential for pollution during processing and manufacture. During expansion, some foams release various chemicals into the atmosphere, most of which are relatively harmless. Polyicynene foam

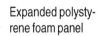

Expanded polystyrene foam panel

releases carbon dioxide as it expands, and expanded polystyrene releases pentane gas. Another issue concerning foams is the waste or excess foam created during manufacture or installation. Most foam materials do not deteriorate readily when disposed of, possibly lasting one hundred years or more. If foam products are used, waste disposal or recycling should be a priority. It should be stated that foams are some of the very best insulators available.

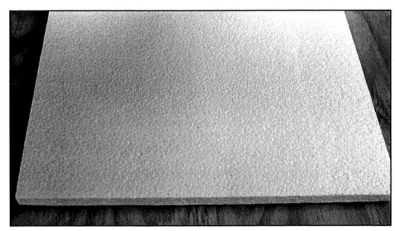

Cellulose insulation

Sealants and
adhesives

Cellulose Insulation

Cellulose insulation is being used in many new homes. Cellulose is manufactured mainly (75% or more) from recycled newspapers, and is then treated with a flame retardant and insect repellant. Because of this, cellulose insulation is considered to be environmentally friendly. Cellulose insulation manufacture takes advantage of a previously consumed product, and removes that discarded product from the waste stream. The manufacture of cellulose insulation utilizes electrically driven hammer mills; a process that consumes far less energy (50 to 100 times less) than is used to manufacture other insulation materials. Cellulose insulation is energy efficient from a manufacturing standpoint, and provides efficient insulation for the home. The R-value of cellulose is about R-3.6 per inch. There are two general ways in which cellulose insulation is installed in a home. A netting material can be installed over the interior wall studs, and the insulation is blown into these spaces in dry form, another option is to blow the material onto the walls using water as a binding agent. The excess insulation is shaved off of the wall cavities and recycled. Cellulose is also blown in dry form into ceilings. Cellulose insulation applied at the required density will also reduce convective heat losses in a building; standard fiberglass is less efficient at preventing this type of heat loss. Cellulose insulation will last as long as the home.

Sealants and Adhesives

Most sealants and adhesives are manufactured using petroleum derivatives; these products have the same pollution potential as other petroleum based products. Most sealants and adhesives are considered hazardous because of their chemical makeup. Care should be taken in their disposal, and they should never be sent to a landfill in liquid or uncured form. The use of solvents and adhesives can affect indoor air quality of the home, but this is generally a short-term problem as the solvents in the sealing compounds off-gas during curing. Chemically sensitive people should pay special attention to the use of these materials in the construction of their home. Careful attention should be paid to the manufacturers label of any sealant or adhesive.

Alternative Materials

There are alternative building products to those previously discussed. Some of these alternatives have a higher initial cost, but may have specific advantages. Some of these building materials are not new to the building trade, although they may not be common or well known in certain areas. Alternatives are just that, alternatives. These alternative materials may have both, benefits and drawbacks associated with their use. Care and research should be taken whenever choosing an alternative building material.

Insulated Concrete Forms

Insulated concrete forms (ICFs) are an insulating foam form that is stacked up, and filled with concrete to create a wall. The forms are usually made from expanded polystyrene foam. As far as environmental issues, these forms combine the characteristics of both materials (EPS and concrete). Once the

Insulated concrete forms

forms are in place, they should last a very long time (100 years), and emit or off-gas very few chemicals into the home. The forms are also excellent insulators, saving energy, and they reduce air infiltration in the home. Saving this energy will in turn save on the burning of fossil fuels used to power electricity manufacturing plants. ICFs make very strong walls, making homes built with them very safe; they can also reduce the amount of external noise entering the home. Building with ICFs is 10 to 20 percent more expensive than a standard stick-framed home.

Manufactured
lumber I-joist

Structural insulated
panels

Manufactured Lumber

Manufactured lumber is made from formerly undesirable small-diameter, fast growing trees; aspen and poplar trees are two species used for this purpose. These materials are reduced to wood chips, and bonded together with phenol resins using heat and immense pressure. There are many types of manufactured lumber products; load-bearing beams, dimensional lumber, I-joist, and oriented strand board are all examples. The manufacture of these products releases heat, chemicals, and carbon dioxide into the atmosphere. Tree harvesting also creates some pollution. These products make use of timber cut specifically for this purpose, which would otherwise be unusable. These materials also use a larger portion of the tree during manufacture than is utilized in making standard lumber. Manufacturing standard dimensional lumber may utilize only 40% or 50% of a tree, while manufactured lumber will utilize 65% to 75% of a tree. Most manufactured lumber products are designed for a special purpose for, which make it more efficient in that application than standard lumber. Beams can be made to carry larger loads than is possible with conventional lumber, while floor joists are lighter and span greater distances. Other manufactured lumber products, similar to standard 2″ lumber, are not yet cost efficient when compared to standard lumber, but this gap is closing. Waste from these products is treated the same as any other lumber, but you need to be aware that all of these products use resins in their manufacture. Manufactured lumber has a life span similar to standard lumber.

Structural Insulated Panels

Structural insulated panels (SIPs) are composite sandwich panels made of oriented strand board (OSB) as the outside layers with a foam core. The types of foams used in SIP manufacture are polyisocyanate foams or EPS (expanded polystyrene). The panels are very strong and can be used for walls, floors, or roof systems. SIPs can be manufactured in various thicknesses, resulting in different insulation and strength values. These panels do not off-gas, however chemically sensitive people should be cautious. SIPs significantly reduce air infiltration, which improves overall energy efficiency. SIP buildings are more costly than stick-framed buildings (10% to 20% more), however, they are much more energy efficient. Pollution potential from this product comes from the component materials (OSB, foam, adhesives). Because the panels are cut to size in a factory, waste may be recycled or used to make smaller components. SIPs used as structural elements should last 100 years.

Steel Framing Materials

Steel framing has been used in commercial buildings for many years. Steel studs are mainly manufactured from recycled steel products, reusing a waste product, but also use huge amounts of fossil fuels in their manufacture, which releases heat and carbon dioxide into the atmosphere. Steel studs are now considerably cheaper than wood studs (30% cheaper or more). An advantage to steel studs is the fact that they are all perfectly straight, which makes them great for framing non-load bearing interior walls. Some builders are now building entire homes with steel framing, exterior walls, interior walls, and the roof system (load bearing and non-load bearing walls). Building with steel framing will increase construction costs 5% to 10% over a similar wood framed structure. Effectively insulating a steel frame building is more difficult than with other building materials because steel transfers heat more efficiently. A steel framed home should last more than 100 years under normal conditions.

Steel framing

71

Concrete roof tiles

Concrete Roofing Tiles

Concrete roofing tiles are an excellent alternative to organic based asphalt shingles or clay tiles. Concrete tiles are similar to clay tiles in that they are heavy, and last a very long time. Some manufacturers warrant concrete tiles for 50 years. These roof tiles have the same manufacturing issues of all concrete products, but once manu- factured, are virtually inert. Concrete tiles make an excellent roofing material, mainly because of their longevity. One downside to concrete tiles is that they cost about $500 per square, (10' by 10' area of roof) installed. The installation system is slightly different than other roofing systems, in that a wood lattice grid must be nailed to the roof to provide attachment points for the tile.

Steel Roofing Shingles

Steel roofing shingles

Another roofing option is steel roofing shingles. These are steel panels formed to resemble large asphalt shingles, and may be covered with an aggregate similar to that used on asphalt shingles. These steel shingles are normally made from recycled steel. Again, recycled steel is more environmentally friendly than virgin steel, however there are huge amounts of energy used in their manufacture. Steel shingles do have a long life span, 30 to 50 years, and most manufacturers offer a lifetime warranty on this product. These shingles are installed in a manner similar to that of concrete roofing tiles, attached to a wood lattice grid on the roof.

Standing Seam Metal Roofing

Yet another option for roofing is standing seam metal roofing, which has been used on commercial (and some residential) buildings for many years. The product is generally manufactured of steel alloys, and comes with a baked enamel finish. Standing seam roofing is a very low maintenance material, and has a very long life span. One downside to this product is the visual appearance, as this roofing system does not look like any other type of roofing material commonly used on residential homes. Pollution aspects of this material are like that of any metal product.

Standing seam roofing

Rubber Roofing Shingles

Another roofing material is rubber roofing shingles, which is a relatively new product. Rubber shingles are manufactured from recycled manufacturing waste. The waste rubber materials are melted and molded to resemble slate shingles. These rubber shingles are flexible, and can be installed by any professional roofer. Rubber roofing shingles are hail resistant, rated for high winds; look great, and cost about the same as cedar roofing shingles. The product comes with a 50-year warranty but may last longer. Rubber roofing shingles are manufactured from recycled materials, removing those materials from the waste stream, but do require the use of fossil fuels in the manufacturing process.

Rubber roofing tiles

Fiber-cement Siding

Fiber-cement siding is a long lasting siding alternative. This product is manufactured with lightweight Portland cement, sand, and wood fibers to form siding clapboards. These clapboards can last 50 years or more, because they will not rot, burn, warp, and are resistant to impact. Fiber-cement siding has been around for many years, yet is only starting to gain wide spread acceptance in the United States. Fiber cement siding does require painting, however a well-applied paint

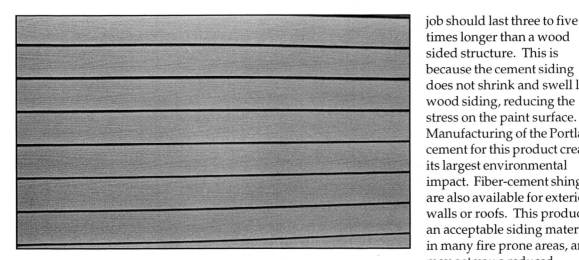

Fiber cement
siding

job should last three to five times longer than a wood sided structure. This is because the cement siding does not shrink and swell like wood siding, reducing the stress on the paint surface. Manufacturing of the Portland cement for this product creates its largest environmental impact. Fiber-cement shingles are also available for exterior walls or roofs. This product is an acceptable siding material in many fire prone areas, and may get you a reduced insurance rate on your home.

Straw Bales

Straw bales are a building material. Straw has been used as structural building component in residential buildings for more than 200 years in Europe, 100 years in the U.S.A. Straw comes from the stalks of cereal grain plants. When

Straw bales

the grain is harvested, the straw is discarded as a waste product, the majority of which is burned in the field. The burning of straw generates huge amounts of smoke, heat, and carbon dioxide. A small portion of the straw is gathered and bailed for a variety of uses; one of these uses can be home construction. Straw bales are stacked up to form the exterior walls of the home. Straw bale walls can be made to support the roof structure, or are integrated into a post & beam building as wall panels. Once in place, the straw walls are covered, inside and outside, with stucco or plaster to keep them dry. The advantages of a straw bale home are that it can be inexpensive to build, it reuses an agricultural waste product, and straw bale buildings have high insulation values. A straw bale wall can have an insulation value between R-25 and R-45, depending upon the type of bale used. Straw has no nutritional value, so it will not attract insects. As long as the straw walls are kept dry, they should have a life span of 100 years or more. Straw bales will probably never become a mainstream building material but they are a viable building option.

Bamboo

Bamboo can be used as an alternative to domestic hardwood flooring. Bamboo is typically used as a flooring material, although bamboo panels are available. Bamboo is technically a grass, much like the grass growing in your yard, but grows in very tall, hollow stalks. It takes about 4 years for a bamboo plant to mature to the point where it can be harvested. Once cut, the bamboo plant re-grows from the roots, and is ready for re-harvesting in another 4 years. Bamboo plants also spread out by their root system to grow new plants. Once harvested, the bamboo is cut into strips that are laminated together to form a board. Currently, almost all bamboo is grown in Asia, and is imported into the United States. Bamboo makes a relatively hard flooring material, having about the same density as oak; however, material density will vary depending on plant variety and manufacturing process. Bamboo is available in both finished and unfinished form. Not all bamboo flooring is of the same quality, and caution should be taken when purchasing this product. Bamboo flooring can be refinished, and should last the lifetime of your home.

Bamboo flooring

When deciding what materials to use in home construction, you have to weigh the benefits against the detriments for each product. You need to consider the cost of the product, the appearance, how long it will last, how much maintenance will be required, and how the product impacts the environment. You may choose to use environmentally sustainable products extensively in your home, or you may use them sparingly. The next few pages contain a chart rating various building materials; this rating takes into account the criteria above. Appendix C has a long list of Internet web sites with information about many of the building materials previously discussed. You will also find an assortment of web links at www.futurehomestoday.com. Take some time and investigate you options.

Building Material Energy Efficiency & Environmental Impact

	Manufacturing Energy Efficiency	Structure Energy Efficiency	Renewability of Components	Raw Resource Availability	Construction Efficiency	Material Cost Efficiency	Material Life Span	Reduced Maintenance Requirements	Occupant Protection	Reduced Occupant Health Risk	Social Acceptance	Material Point Totals - "higher is better"
Structural Components												
Dimensional Lumber	3	2	2	3	5	5	3	3	1	5	5	3.7
Manufactured Lumber	2	2	3	4	5	3	3	3	1	4	5	3.5
Concrete	3	1	1	5	4	3	5	4	5	5	5	4.1
Insulated Concrete Forms	3	5	1	4	4	2	5	4	5	4	5	4.2
Structural Insulated Panels	3	5	3	3	5	2	3	3	2	4	4	3.7
Straw Bale	5	5	5	5	4	5	3	3	1	5	1	4.2
Steel Frame	2	2	1	4	4	3	4	3	1	5	4	3.3
Exterior Sheathing												
Composite Wood Siding	3	2	3	3	4	5	2	1	1	5	4	3.3
Stucco	3	1	1	5	4	3	4	3	1	5	5	3.5
Brick	2	1	1	5	3	3	5	5	3	5	5	3.8
Stone	4	1	1	5	2	2	5	5	3	5	5	3.8
Vinyl Siding	3	2	1	2	5	5	2	3	1	5	4	3.3
Wood Clapboard	3	2	2	2	3	2	4	2	1	5	5	3.1
Aluminum Siding	2	2	1	2	4	4	2	4	1	5	4	3.1
Fiber Cement Siding	3	1	2	5	4	4	4	4	2	5	5	3.9

Building Material Energy Efficiency & Environmental Impact

Material	Manufacturing Energy Efficiency	Structure Energy Efficiency	Renewability of Components	Raw Resource Availability	Construction Efficiency	Material Cost Efficiency	Material Life Span	Reduced Maintenance Requirements	Occupant Protection	Reduced Occupant Health Risk	Social Acceptance	Material Point Totals - "higher is better"
Roofing Materials												
Asphalt Shingles	3	2	1	2	5	5	2	3	3	4	5	3.5
Wood Shakes	3	3	2	2	3	3	3	3	2	3	5	3.2
Cement Roofing Tiles	3	2	2	4	4	3	5	5	4	4	4	4
Clay Tile	2	2	2	4	4	3	5	5	4	4	4	3.9
Cement Fiber Shakes	3	2	2	4	4	3	5	5	4	4	4	4
Steel Roofing Shingles	2	3	1	3	5	4	5	5	3	4	3	3.8
Rubber Roofing Shingles	3	2	1	2	5	3	3	4	3	4	3	3.5
Standing Seam Roofing	3	3	1	3	5	4	5	5	4	4	3	4
Miscellaneous Materials												
Carpeting	3	3	3	4	5	5	2	2	3	2	5	3.7
Ceramic Tile	3	3	3	5	3	3	5	4	3	4	4	4
Vinyl Tile	3	3	2	3	4	4	4	3	3	3	4	3.5
Bamboo Flooring	4	3	5	4	3	3	4	4	3	4	3	4
Fiberglass Insulation	3	4	3	4	5	5	4	3	3	3	5	4.2
Cellulose Insulation	5	5	4	5	5	5	4	3	3	4	4	4.6
Foam Insulation	3	5	2	3	4	4	4	3	3	3	3	3.6
Soft Plywood	3	2	2	3	5	5	3	3	1	4	5	3.6
Oriented Strand Board	3	2	4	4	5	5	3	3	1	4	5	3.9

4   Construction Methods

There are several conventional construction methods in use today for residential and commercial buildings. These methods meet the building codes in virtually every state, county, and city in the country. These building methods are efficient from a construction standpoint, but not so efficient from a resource conservation or energy efficiency standpoint. There are improvements that can be made to existing building methods, and there are alternative building methods that can be more efficient in these areas, and potentially in the area of construction efficiency.

Conventional Construction Methods

There are several basic methods of construction in use today. For residential homes the two main methods are wood framing (stick-framing), and masonry (concrete block or poured concrete walls). Both of these have been in use for many years, and have proven to be cost effective and structurally sound.

Wood framing consists of using dimensional lumber to form a vertical grid structure, providing vertical support, while a sheet product (plywood or OSB) provides lateral strength (support from side to side). The roofing system is then placed upon this vertical structure to form a building. A siding product (vinyl, wood clapboards, stucco, etc.) covers the exterior of the building, the interior wall cavities are filled with an insulating material (fiberglass, cellulose, etc.), and the interior walls are covered with a sheathing product such as

Wood frame walls and roof trusses

gypsum wallboard. This system forms a solid structure that can be constructed relatively quickly, and at reasonable cost. Stick-framed homes, as we know them, have been in existence since the 1880s, when dimensional lumber became readily available from lumberyards. A wood frame home can easily last more than 100 years if it is on a good foundation, and is properly maintained.

There are a few problems with stick-framed construction. First, the quality of lumber available for construction is decreasing. This has been the case for the past several decades, because over 95% of the old growth forests (the source of the best lumber) have been harvested in the United States. As the higher quality wood in old growth forest is depleted, lumber companies have begun to harvest trees of lesser quality. Trees that would have been discarded as unusable in the past are now harvested, and turned into dimensional lumber. Trees re-grown for harvest, 2nd and 3rd growth forests, have far less competition for resources, and grow much faster because of ample water, fertilizer, and space. This creates lesser quality wood that is more prone to warp out of shape, and which makes it more difficult to build a straight, sturdy structure. The cost of lumber of all types has also increased significantly in the past few decades. This is in part the result of more homes being built, thus more competition for lumber resources. Also, the cost of lumber production is continually increasing because of workers wage demands, equipment costs, insurance costs, transportation costs, etc.

The second main problem with stick-framed buildings is the insulation value of the construction material. The dimensional lumber that makes up the structure of the building creates a solid block of wood from the outside to the interior. Wood is not a wonderful insulator, not nearly as efficient as fiberglass insulation, having approximately one-third the insulation value of standard fiberglass insulation. This wooden structure creates a channel or bridge for heat to travel into or out of the home. There are ways to build the structure to reduce this problem. You can build double wall exterior walls, staggering the studs of these walls in order to

Wood framed building under construction

effectively break the heat transfer path, but doubles the cost of the exterior shell. There are also sheathing products that you can apply to the outside of the building to increase insulation value, this method does help to reduce heat loss but will also increase building costs.

A third problem with stick-framing is the numerous cavities created by this construction method. The structural frame of a stick-framed building creates cavities in the walls, which are difficult to insulate and seal uniformly. Standard fiberglass insulation fills the bulk of the cavities, yet leaves many small spaces will no insulation. If there are un-insulated spaces left in a wall through which air can travel (air infiltration), the thermal efficiency of the building suffers. There are products available that greatly reduce air infiltration called air infiltration barriers. Air infiltration barriers are installed over the exterior vertical walls of the building, behind the exterior siding. These barriers are designed to slow the rate at which air can blow into, and through small openings in walls. Reducing the airflow through a building reduces the heat transfer into or out of the building, increasing thermal efficiency. Air infiltration barriers do allow water vapor to pass through them to the outdoors; this is important because you do not want water vapor trapped inside of the walls, saturating the insulation product. Even with an air infiltration barrier, you will still have un-insulated cavities in the frame walls, which will allow for uncontrolled heat transfer, decreasing the energy efficiency of the house. Careful installation of the insulating material can help eliminate some of these problems. This subject is covered in detail in the chapter 5 of this book.

Yet another issue with wood framed homes is the fact that there is a limited amount of insulation that can be placed in the wall cavities. The standard insulation value for a 2"x4" wall is R-13, a 2"x6" wall can be insulated to a

Fiberglass insulation is used in most homes

value of R-19. The lack of insulation space in these walls limits the energy efficiency of the building. There are other building products that offer much higher insulation values, which reduce building energy consumption.

Beyond energy issues, there are still other issues concerning wood framed housing. The potential of damage from termites or carpenter ants to a wooden structure can be a concern, but these can be controlled with pesticides. The survivability of a stick-framed

home in the event of severe weather is questionable. Wood frame homes can withstand all but the most severe weather such as tornadoes and hurricanes. In the case of such weather, you will need a more secure area to escape to, such as a safe room. Wood framed homes, like most homes, are also susceptible to fire damage.

There are common building practices used for a stick-frame home construction throughout the country, but there are alternative stick-framing methods that address, and partially solve some of the issues previously discussed.

Programs like "Build America" promote the use of advanced framing methods.

One advanced framing method uses larger exterior wall studs (2"x6" as opposed to 2"x4"), and spaces the wall studs further apart (24" as opposed to 16"). This accomplishes two things. First, the larger studs spaced further apart, allowing for the installation of more insulation in the wall cavities creating a more energy efficient wall structure; second, this method reduces the amount of wood used to build the home. This framing method uses less wood, because the larger lumber, spaced further apart, results in fewer board feet of lumber used in the construction of the home (board feet is a unit of measuring a quantity of different dimension lumber). Less wood means fewer trees cut down to make the lumber. Although these are small steps, they are positive steps.

Masonry

Textured concrete block wall

There are several different types of masonry construction available, the most common material for above ground structures being concrete blocks or concrete masonry units (CMU). Other options are poured concrete walls or stone & mortar walls. Masonry walls provide a strong, safe, stable structure for a

home, which is why masonry construction is used so extensively in hurricane prone areas. If placed on a good foundation, a masonry wall should last long time. Well over one hundred years. Buildings in Europe of masonry construction are centuries old. Virtually no brick or stone homes built today are constructed with solid masonry walls; instead brick and stone are used as a veneer or surface covering, and not as a structural element. Solid brick walls are no longer used to build homes because the cost of materials, the cost of labor, and a lack of thermal efficiency make this method of construction too expensive and inefficient. Masonry veneers do provide a long lasting, low maintenance exterior surface for the home.

With masonry structures, strength is usually not a problem; the biggest problem with masonry walls is energy efficiency. It is difficult to build an energy efficient structure of masonry products, because they have almost no insulation value. If you build a masonry building in a climate with cold winter temperatures, you will have to take measures to hold the heat inside your building. Masonry construction, both walls and floors, will also readily allow moisture to be transferred through the structure.

Options for insulating the building include: foam panels applied to the interior or exterior walls, wood framed and insulated walls on the interior, or adding some sort of insulation to the cavities of a block wall.

You can add foam panels to the masonry walls of your home. The foam panels must be fairly thick in order to provide adequate insulation value to the masonry wall. Foam panels have an insulation value of about R-3.6 per inch. This means you need at least 3" of foam to attain a minimal insulation value.

Poured concrete basement walls and floor

The foam panels must also be fitted closely together, and the seams sealed with tape or an expanding foam sealant to insure good energy efficiency. This does create a small problem is you intend to attach a sheathing material on top of the foam panels, because foam panels are very light weight, and may not have the structural strength necessary to support a sheathing material. If you put up nailing strips to support the finish material, and then put foam in-between the spaces, you compromise the effectiveness of

the insulation because of the low insulation R-value of the nailing strips, and the voids created between the foam panels and the nailing strips.

In concrete block walls, you can fill the block cavities with insulation, which increases the R-value of the wall, but there remain efficient pathways for the transfer of heat through the mortar joints and block webs. Block walls are cost effective, strong, and safe, but they are not energy efficient. The only real way to improve the thermal efficiency of masonry walls is to build a different type of wall system inside the structure to provide thermal efficiency, or to add a solid layer of insulation material to the wall. This works, but it dramatically increases the construction cost.

Alternative Building Methods

Today there are several alternative building materials that provide excellent thermal efficiency, but are not widely used in residential construction. Some of these materials are also more ecologically sound than the building materials previously discussed. These alternate materials include insulated concrete forms, structural insulated panels, and straw bale construction. The goals of alternative building materials are: to provide a safe, strong building at reasonable cost, provide high energy efficiency, and to have reasonable ecological soundness.

Insulated Concrete Forms

Insulated concrete forms have been used in Europe for some time, but they have only recently become an option for residential and commercial construction in this country. Insulated concrete forms (ICFs) are available in several different configurations from a number of manufacturers. In general, ICFs are two thick foam panels, held apart by a plastic or metal separator, forming a space between the panels. This separator or webbing passes from one outside surface of the form to the other outside surface of the form, providing the fastening point for sheathing products on both the inside and outside walls of the building. Each foam panel is about 3" thick with the space between the panels being about 6", making a building block measuring approximately 2 feet tall, by 4 feet wide, by 12 inches deep. These foam building blocks are stacked together at the building site to form a wall. Reinforcing metal bars (rebar) are placed in the hollow space of the forms, which are then filled with concrete to create a solid wall. The concrete provides the support structure of the wall, and the foam provides the insulation value. An ICF wall will provide an insulation value of about R-25 to R-30, which is a higher insulation value than many other building products. The foam itself is typically made with expanded polystyrene (EPS) foam. Two additional advantages of ICFs are that the walls are extremely strong (solid concrete structure inside the form), and there are no voids in the walls to allow air infiltration. The inability of air to transfer through the wall greatly adds to the overall thermal efficiency of the building (remember the problems with wood framed buildings, and the many potential places for air infiltration and heat transfer).

Insulated concrete form

ICFs can be used to build walls for the basement, 1st floor, or 2nd floor. If they are used for the basement walls or any walls below grade, they need to be sealed to prevent water penetration, and protected from being damaged when the foundation is back filled (back filling is when the dirt removed for building the foundation is replaced). Standard, below grade, water protection systems are applicable. Building codes specific to your area should be followed when using ICFs for the structural elements of a home. The manufacturer of the forms will be able to provide specific information as to building practices when using this product. Channels for installing electrical wiring can be cut into interior or exterior foam surfaces of the completed wall assembly with an electric hot knife. After any mechanical components are installed, the walls can be sheathed or covered, both interior and exterior, as with any other building material.

ICF wall, filled with concrete during construction

There are additional advantages to building a home with ICFs. They create a very quiet building (will you be building near an interstate, a busy street, or under the airport flight path?), because the foam and concrete walls absorb and dampen noises from outside the home. They also form a strong building, because you end up with a 6" thick, steel reinforce, concrete wall surrounding your home. The strength of an ICF home can be important in the event of severe weather, such as a tornado or hurricane. ICF walls can also be used as interior walls for support, interior sound separation, or to build a safe room. Building with ICFs costs about 10% more than building a wood frame home with 2"x6" exterior walls, or 20% more than a home framed with standard 2"x4" lumber. This increased building cost can be recouped in energy savings over time. There are several web addresses of ICF manufacturers in the appendix of this book.

Structural Insulated Panels

Another building option is Structural Insulated Panels (SIPs). An SIP is a factory made panel consisting of a foam core sandwiched between two skins of OSB sheathing. The foam core is usually made of polyisocyanate foam or expanded polystyrene foam. Standard sizes are 4' by 8', but SIPs can be built to almost any dimension, the only limitation being the size of panel that can be transported to the building site, and set into place by hand or with a crane.

SIPs are also available in various thicknesses, the thicker the panel, the greater the insulating value. SIPs can be used for flooring structures, vertical walls, or as roof panels; their uses are only limited by the imagination of the designer, and the manufacturing facilities of the panel provider. SIPs can only be used in above ground construction.

Since SIPs are manufactured in a factory to design specifications (specific to the house being built), the panels are cut to size to allow them to fit tightly together as they are assembled at the building site. Once made, they can then be transported to the building site, and erected very quickly. This

Structrual insulated panels can be used for walls, roofs, and floors

can be advantageous if you have concerns of poor weather during the construction process. The panels are usually joined by a mechanical means (screws or nails), the joints being filled with expanding foam to insure a

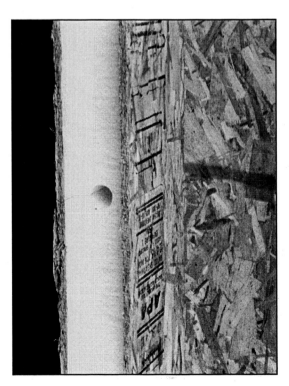

consistent insulation value through the wall. SIPs can provide insulating values of about R-20 to R-40, although some manufacturers may be able to offer panels with higher insulation values (thicker panels). SIPs are generally used for the exterior walls but can also be used for interior walls. There are many different manufactures of SIPs, all with slight variations of construction techniques. Most SIPs have wiring channels formed into the panels to ease the process of installing electrical, telephone, and cable wiring in the walls. The exterior and interior surfaces of SIP structures can be covered with standard siding and sheathing materials.

Manufacturers of SIPs claim that a home built with their products are considerably stronger than stick-framed homes. This is achieved because the wall panels form a single, composite unit, providing both vertical support and sheer load support. SIPs are quite strong, but may not stop the flying debris created during a tornado or hurricane. SIPs also provide an effective barrier against air infiltration, because the panels have a solid foam core, and there are no spaces to allow air to pass through the material. This, combined with the high insulation value of the foam core, allows for the construction of very energy efficient buildings. There are higher building costs associated with SIPs compared to standard stick-framed homes (about a 20% increase). This higher cost can be recouped in energy savings if you stay in the home long enough. The appendix of this book has the web address of SIPA (Structural Insulated Panel Association), which has a listing of all the SIP manufacturers in the country.

Straw Bale Construction

Yet another viable alternative building material for energy efficient homes are straw bales. This building method makes more sense than you may think at first. Don't believe the story about the three little pigs. There are examples of straw bale buildings more than 200 years old in Europe, and there are 100-year-old straw buildings on the Great Plains of the U.S.A. Straw is a residual waste product, the stalk of the plant, from the harvesting of cereal grains such as wheat, and rice. Building with straw is environmentally friendly in several ways, because it is essentially a waste product of farming that is either left on the ground to decay, or is burned. The process of burning straw in the field releases huge amounts of smoke and carbon dioxide into the atmosphere. Building homes from straw removes this waste product from the environment, puts it into productive use, and reduces the amount of lumber used in the construction of new homes.

Straw bale home under construction

There are two sizes of straw bales available, 3 string bales, and 2 string bales. 3 string bales are larger, approximately 23" x 18" x 55", these bales will have an R-value of about R-40 across the width of the bale when laid flat (23"). This equals an R-value of about 1.7 per inch. 2 string bales are approximately 16" x 14" x 40", and will provide about an R-28 insulation value across the width. The R-value is actually higher across the height of the bales if they are turned 90 degrees (this is called laid on edge), because the hollow stalks create better air spaces in this direction, having an R-value of about R-2.5 per inch. It is important that load bearing walls not be made with the bales laid on edge because they compress too much. Straw bale homes save energy by the nature of their low energy consumption in the manufacture of the base product, and the inherent insulation value in the finished structure.

There are two methods of building straw bale houses. The first is to support the roof system in some way such as a post & beam structure, pole barn, etc. The second method is to have the straw bale walls themselves support the roof system, and is called "Nebraska style". The first method, though slightly more expensive, will probably create a longer lasting and safer building, because the weight of the roof is borne by wooden, vertical supports. In a load bearing straw bale structure, it may take 8 weeks for the bales to settle, or compress to their relative final state. Heavy snow loads can further compress the walls after the building has been completed, causing problems and cracking the finished wall surfaces. In general, the cost of constructing a straw bale home can be much less than when using more conventional construction materials, with many straw bale homes being constructed by "do-it-yourself" type builders for as little as $5 to $50 per square foot. There are also straw bale homes built by professional construction companies, which can cost more than homes built with contemporary materials ($50 to $200 per square foot). Besides energy efficiency, another advantage to a straw bale home is that it is very quiet. The thickness of the material allows it to absorb and dampen sounds coming from the outside environment. This makes the interior of the home quiet and peaceful. Straw bale homes can last many years; there are examples of straw bale structures in Nebraska that are more than one hundred years old.

Stucco being applied to a straw bale home

Straw bale walls are erected on top of a foundation/flooring system, usually of concrete. The bales are stacked to the desired height to form a wall, each row of bales being tied together using wooden or steel stakes, driven down through the bales. The bales are arranged in a staggered manner, much like concrete blocks in a masonry structure. Smaller bales are made on the site to fill in any odd spaces around doors, windows, or at corners. There are limits to the length of unsupported wall that can be built using straw bales, and there is a limit to wall height. These limitations exist, because unsupported straw bale walls lack strength in certain directions. Very strong winds might blow down an unsupported wall that is too long or too high. This issue is easily overcome with proper design. Openings for windows and doors can be made by incorporating a square wooden form into the wall, and attaching it to the bales with metal lath. This frame provides support for the bales above the opening, and a nailing surface to which the doors and windows are attached. A supporting header may need to be incorporated into the frame of larger door or window openings. Roof systems for straw bale homes are the same as those used in conventional construction.

Straw bale walls must be kept dry before, during, and after construction. Special measures should be taken to ensure the straw stays dry for the life of the house. The first place to protect is the location where the bales are placed upon the foundation. Because the concrete foundation allows water to be transferred through it, there needs to be an effective, and long lasting water barrier at this location. The walls of a straw bale house are typically covered in stucco or plaster both inside and outside, which prevents water from reaching the bales, causing them to decay. Again, care must be taken to completely seal the bales from the weather, paying special attention around doors and windows. Straw bale homes are not any more attractive to insects than are conventional homes. This is because the straw has no nutritional value, so insects will not eat the straw itself.

There are several books on the subject of straw bale buildings, and "hands-on" seminars are also available in some parts of the country. Straw bale buildings are gaining acceptance in some parts of the country, mainly the southwest and west. You should check with local building officials before planning to build a straw home, their building codes might not address this type of construction. You may even need to educate the building code authorities in your area in order for them to allow you to build a straw bale home. In the appendix of this book you will find a list of several straw building books, and several web site addresses regarding the subject.

A finished straw bale home

The three alternative building materials listed above provide high insulation values with little opportunity for air infiltration through the wall materials. All of these materials can be considered "Super Insulators" from their high R-values. Some problems associated with super-insulated homes are discussed in a subsequent chapter.

Steel Frame Construction

Steel framed homes are another building option, and can be framed completely of steel components, manufactured specifically for that purpose. The majority of the steel framing materials are made from recycled steel. Steel stud walls have been used for many years in the commercial construction industry, and are now beginning to be used in residential homes. Today, non-load bearing, steel studs are less expensive than standard 2"x4" lumber. The steel studs have another advantage, they are always perfectly straight, and the will not warp like wood.

In the past few years the steel industry has begun to develop and promote building homes entirely of steel. The exterior walls of steel homes are generally 6" or more in thickness, which allows for more insulation to be placed in the walls as opposed to most wood framed homes. The exterior walls are also constructed with fewer vertical members than is typically used in wood frame construction, this also allows for more insulation to be placed in the wall cavities. A series of horizontal runners are attached to the vertical supports

Steel frame wall

inside and outside of the frame, and serve two purposes; they provide fastening points for interior and exterior siding, and they reduce the area for heat transfer through the walls.

Steel is a metal, and thus is an excellent conductor of heat, but this is bad if you want to hold heat inside a home. To limit this heat transfer potential, the attachment points for the horizontal runners are small (approximately 1/2" square). This small size limits the ability of the steel frame to transfer the heat through the wall.

Heat loss with a steel frame building should still be a concern. Adding exterior insulating sheathing to the exterior of the building can help to further reduce heat loss, however, this will increase your construction cost.

Steel frame homes cost about 20% more than a stick-framed home. An advantage of steel framed homes is that insects such as termites cannot damage the supporting structure of the home. Termites will still eat other materials in the home such as the paper on drywall sheathing, and any wood used in the home for other purposes. Another concern is that steel buildings do not stand-up well to fire, although steel does not burn, it does weaken rapidly when exposed to extreme heat. Fire may weaken the frame, causing the structure to collapse more quickly than a wooden building. Wood on the other hand does not weaken in fire from the heat; wood must partially burn through before it collapses.

Modular Homes

Another building option is a modular or factory built home. Most people think of a modular home as an unattractive trailer-type building, this may have been true in the past, but today the design and construction of modular homes is much more versatile. Modular homes come in all shapes, sizes, and price ranges, even portions of expensive homes are being built in factories, trucked to the building site, and assembled. This type of manufacture offers some advantages over a site built home.

Since modular homes are built in a factory, they are not affected by inclement weather, the construction of the home continues on a daily basis, rain or shine.

Modular homes are becoming a viable housing option

Modular homes can also be less expensive than traditionally built frame homes. This is because the factory purchases the building materials in huge quantities at a discount, and these savings are transferred to the homebuyer. Another advantage of a modular home is a higher level of quality control possible in a factory, because the same work crews construct the homes on a weekly basis, and quality inspectors can closely watch the construction process. If there is a

quality problem, it can be identified, corrected, and eliminated in the next home. There is also less waste produced by a factory built home, because small scraps, (normally discarded) can be utilized in other ways as additional homes are built. Materials that can be reclaimed include most wood scraps, flooring, electrical wiring, insulation, and more. Not all of these scraps will end up in another home, but they may be used as heating fuel for the manufacturing plant. The important point is that there will be less waste generated by a factory built home than a site built home.

There are some disadvantages to factory built homes. The first may be availability in your area. Because the homes are built in a factory, it must be transported to its future site. Transporting a home over a long distance is very expensive, so most modular home manufactures will be in close proximity to large metropolitan areas. If you live in a remote area, a modular home may be more expensive than a home built on your site. A quality modular home should last as long as any stick-framed home, and since virtually all modular homes are stick-framed. They will only be as energy efficient as similarly constructed homes. The quality, variety, and availability of modular homes is continually improving, you may want to investigate this option for your home.

Reclaimed Lumber

Another alternative building method is not really an alternative. Recycled old growth timbers are of high quality, and their reuse is environmentally sound. One hundred years ago, before the use of steel in commercial construction became common, huge timbers were used to construct commercial buildings. Many of these buildings exist today as abandoned factories or warehouses. As these buildings are torn down, the lumber used in their construction can be recycled into many useful forms. Recycled into ceiling or floor joists, flooring boards, wall panels, timbers for timber frame homes, furniture, etc. Most of this wood is of higher quality than is readily available today. Recycling this wood is good because the resource is reused in new home construction, and new trees do not have to be harvested to make these products. You may be able to find reclaimed lumber, for use in your home, in the yellow pages of your telephone book.

Stick-framed homes can last more than a century

There are yet other alternative building materials available. Rammed earth homes, earth-sheltered homes, and timber-framed homes are just some examples. These methods may be viable options, each with its own advantages and disadvantages. Issues may include problems similar to those with conventional construction methods, viability on a regional basis only, or a lack of acceptance by the general public because of style or building material.

Don't misunderstand the information provided in this chapter, there are millions of good, wood framed and masonry homes in this country. You probably live in one. The point is that there are alternative building materials available, which may provide better solutions. There are always compromises to be made when using an alternative building material. Most of these compromises are out weighed by the advantages of using such a material. The advantages of an alternative building material can be less impact on the environment, higher energy efficiency, a quieter dwelling, a longer lasting structure, and more peace of mind for the builder and the owner.

A point of caution should be raised, one must be careful about choosing an alternative building method or material. Some alternative building methods may seem viable and sound initially, but as a building ages and goes through changes, the end result may have some unforeseen problems. Research and local expertise may prove the difference between a successful home, and a disaster. Thorough investigation of alternative building methods should be performed to prevent problems.

True adobe homes are only practical in some areas of the country

Conventional building methods have been in use for a long time, and most of these methods have evolved considerably during the past century. Conventional methods are efficient and fast but may not be particularly energy efficient, or environmentally sound. As our world changes, so must our habits. At the turn of the century, no one was concerned about the energy efficiency of a home, heating fuels were cheap, and insulating materials were fire hazards, or too expensive. The situation is much different today. The future could hold even more importance for energy efficiency, as energy continues to become more expensive, while our energy supplies continue to dwindle. Who knows what the future holds? More information and web links on this subject are available at www.futurehomestoday.com.

5   Insulation

In any structure, heat flows from warm areas to cooler areas, regardless of the direction (up, down, or sideways). Insulation is a material that resists the flow of heat through it, and thus slows down the passage of heat into or out of a building. This is what the insulation in your home actually does; it insulates the interior of your home from the temperature variations of the climate outside your home by slowing down the heat transfer process.

The transfer of heat occurs in one of three basic ways; these processes can occur by them selves or in any combination of the three.

Conduction - Conduction is the transfer of heat through an object. When one side of an object is heated, the heat will move through the object to the other side. Heat is naturally transferred from areas of high concentration to areas of lower concentration, as it seeks equalization throughout the object. As one side of the object is heated, the molecules in that area begin to move faster, and bump against adjacent molecules, causing them to move, transferring the energy. This process continues, transferring the heat throughout the object. Different materials conduct or transfer heat at different rates.

Heat will flow in any direction to leave your home

Convection - Convection is the transfer of heat through a fluid by the circulation of the fluid; both air and water are considered to be fluids, and transfer heat in this manner. In a wall cavity, air absorbs heat from the warm interior wall, circulates within the wall cavity, and transfers the heat to the colder exterior wall. This convective heat loss cycle occurs continuously if not impeded by an insulating material.

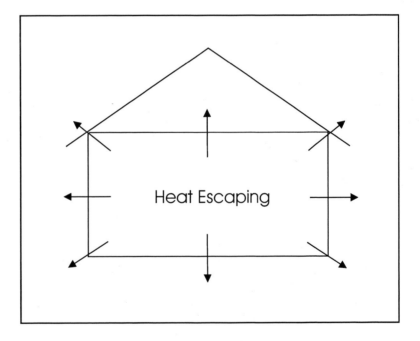

Heat Escaping

Radiation - Radiation occurs when an object is heated; the heated object will radiate heat waves to cooler objects without heating the air between the objects. Heat is transferred in this manner as infrared energy. The earth receives most of its heat from the sun in this manner.

As everyone knows, it is very important to effectively insulate our homes in order to conserve energy. It is important to insulate, and thus separate climate-controlled areas inside the home from the effects of the climate outside the home. This means you must insulate the ceilings, walls, and possibly floors of your home to reduce heat loss.

How does insulation reduce heat loss? Heat is naturally transferred from an area of higher concentration to an area of lower concentration. Materials allow heat to transfer through them at different rates; these different transfer rates are the result of the structure and density of the material. Materials that transfer heat very well generally have no air spaces in their structure. Metal is an example of a material that transfers heat well. Materials that transfer heat poorly generally have many tiny air spaces in their structure. Expanded polystyrene foam is an example of a material that transfers heat poorly; the air spaces in the foam slow down the ability of heat to transfer through the material. Foam is a good insulator because, the air in a cell of the foam must be warmed up, and then transferred through the cell wall to heat up the next cell; this process takes time, and slows down the transfer of heat.

All insulators that are used in home construction have an R-value, which is an insulating efficiency rating of the insulating material. The higher the R-value, the better the insulating efficiency. Wood has an R-value of about R-1 per inch, while fiberglass insulation has an R-value of about R-3.2 per inch. Expanded polystyrene has an R-value of about R-3.7 per inch. Since heat is transferred by conduction, convection, radiation, or a combination of the three, an efficient insulation material must be able to resist heat transfer by any of these methods, or a combination of these methods. The physical properties of the insulating material, and the quality of the installation of that material affect the efficiency.

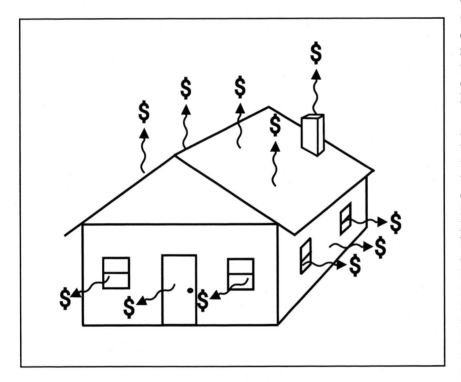

A poorly insulated house looses conditioned air quickly and wastes energy

How do insulating materials resist the three methods of heat transfer? To answer this question, we must look at each method individually.

Conduction is the transfer of heat through an object. To resist this type of heat transfer, insulating materials need to be lightweight, or have a low mass. Lightweight materials, such as fiberglass, do not conduct heat well, where as high mass materials, such as brick, do conduct heat well. The lighter weight a material, generally the better it insulates, but this only applies to conductive heat loss. Materials that are too light or too porous can loose heat by other methods, reducing insulating efficiency.

Convection is the movement of heat in a circulating fluid. If the insulating material is dense enough to resist air movement within the structure of the material, and the insulator is installed properly in the walls of the home, there will be no space for the movement of a fluid (air). If the fluid cannot move, heat loss by convection is virtually eliminated. This is why it is so important to fill all the airspaces in an insulated wall with the insulating material, and to make sure that your insulating material is installed at the density level specified by the manufacturer. Large air cavities in the insulator, or too low of a density allows for convective heat loss.

Radiant heat loss occurs when heat can radiate from one object to another in the form of infrared energy. Because most insulation materials have a cellular structure, the ability of heat to radiate through it is essentially eliminated. The insulation material does not allow the heat absorbed by the inside walls of the home to radiate through the wall cavity to the outside walls and be lost.

Every house continuously looses energy by all three heat transfer methods

During the construction of a home, insulation is normally added to the building. We use insulation materials to reduce the heat loss from our homes, which in turn reduces our energy usage, and associated expenses. Insulation is a relatively inexpensive material when compared to other building materials, but because it has the ability to reduce recurring energy costs, increasing the amount of insulation in

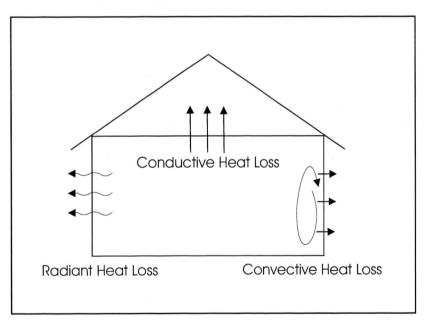

your home can save money in the long term. Most common building materials, such as wood framed and masonry homes require that we add insulation to the physical structure of the home during the construction process, while insulated concrete forms, structural insulated panels, and straw bale homes have insulating qualities in their structure, and do not require the addition of other insulating materials.

How do you choose the insulating material for your home? The R-value is not the only factor in choosing an insulating material. Other factors include the ability of the material to harbor mold or mildew, moisture resistance, attractiveness of the material to vermin and insects, the resistance of the insulator to fire, the cost of the installation, and the environmental impact of the insulating material. There are several different types of insulating products, each with its own properties.

Most people understand that you need to insulate the walls and ceilings in a home. Walls and ceilings form the areas that are typically climate controlled with heating or air conditioning. The insulation helps to keep these spaces conditioned to our satisfaction.

If the walls and ceiling of the home are insulated, heat will travel down-ward to escape

Where people generally overlook insulation is in their floor system. The floor is the other side of the box in which we live. It is generally thought that heat only rises. Heat will rise, and does prefer to travel up in order to escape, however, if you insulate the walls and the ceiling to prevent heat loss, heat will travel through the un-insulated floor to escape. The heat is taking the path of least resistance to find equilibrium with the outdoor climate.

Heat Escaping

Homes are built with three types of flooring systems. The first is the concrete slab floor, which is simply a layer of concrete poured on top of the ground. Slab floors are built where the ground is very rocky, has a high water table, or the cost of the building is an issue. Slabs floors are less expensive than most other flooring systems. Ridged foam insulation, and a plastic vapor barrier should be placed under the concrete slab before it is poured; the foam will help the home retain heat, and the plastic will prevent moisture from entering the home through the floor.

The second type of flooring system is a wood floor with a crawl space beneath. This flooring system usually rests on short foundation walls of concrete block, and is used where the ground is sloped, rocky, or the owners do not want to invest in a basement. This type of flooring system is generally made of ply-wood with wooden flooring joists, providing little insulation value. Insulation of various types can be applied to the bottom side of this type flooring system to help the home retain heat. It is important to seal the openings to the crawl space so that vermin do not make a home in the insulation under your floor.

The third type of flooring system involves a basement under the home. In areas where basements are feasible, many homeowners will make the extra investment in a basement in order to gain the additional space. The flooring system for the 1st floor and the ceiling for the basement are the same, plywood flooring with wooden floor joists. If the basement is not used as a living area and is not climate controlled, insulation can be added beneath the flooring system of the 1st floor in order to reduce heat loss to the basement. Many basements are used as family areas, and are climate controlled. In either case, these areas can be insulated to prevent heat loss into the ground surrounding the basement; ground temperature, below 3 feet, is about 58 degrees in most areas. Basement floors are usually made of concrete, and can be insulated like slab floors, with foam insulation under the floor. Basement walls can be insulated on the exterior, the interior, or both. Again this can be done in order to reduce heat loss to the cooler ground, conserving energy.

The bottom line is that your flooring system can be a major source of energy loss in a home, and should be insulated.

Insulation Materials

The following section details the different types of insulation materials.

Fiberglass Insulation

Fiberglass is used in the vast majority of homes as the insulating material. Fiberglass insulation is just what its name implies, a product manufactured from glass formed into long fibers, and bonded to make insulation in the form of rolls (long rolls of insulation with a paper backing) or batts (4' pieces of insulation with no backing). These insulation rolls or batts are manufactured to fit between the studs of a standard framed house (16" or 24" wide). Fiberglass has an R-value of about R-3.2 per inch. Fiberglass insulation will, in general, not slump or settle after installation, but does not easily form to the odd shapes and spaces in wall cavities. Electrical wiring, plumbing pipes, nails, etc., can

Fiberglass insulation is commonly used in stick-framed homes

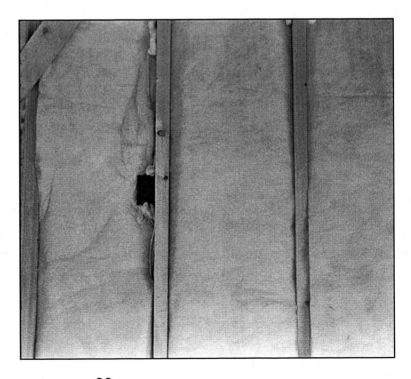

99

cause small gaps or holes in fiberglass insulation; these voids reduce the efficiency of the insulated space. It is critical that fiberglass insulation be installed carefully to avoid as many of these insulation voids as possible. Fiberglass does not support the growth of mold or mildew, but will hold some water if allowed to get wet, reducing its insulating properties. Another issue with standard fiberglass insulation is its vulnerability to convective heat loss, since standard fiberglass does not have a very dense structure. This allows air to slowly circulate through the insulation, setting up a convective heat loss cycle, reducing insulation efficiency. Denser fiberglass insulations are available, however, they are more expensive than the standard product, and are rarely used in residential homes.

Cellulose insulation is an alternative to standard fiberglass insulation

For below grade insulations, glass fiber panels are usually used. These are made of glass fibers, tightly bonded together to form a panel one to two inches in thickness, with a plastic material containing vertical drainage channels bonded to the backside. These panels are placed over the basement waterproofing barrier (material sprayed on the outside of the basement walls to prevent water from coming through the walls). When the glass panel is adhered to the outside of a basement wall, below grade, it serves two purposes: the first to provide insulation between the ground and the basement walls, reducing heat loss, and the second to channel water around the foundation wall to a drain tile system around the building. Removing this water helps to reduce pressure on the basement walls, and helps to prevent cracking of the walls.

Cellulose Insulation

Cellulose insulation is only used in a small portion of new homes today, mainly because fiberglass has been the standard insulation material for so many years. Cellulose insulation is made from shredded newspapers treated with a chemical to resist fire, insects, and the growth of molds and mildew. Cellulose is an environmentally friendly product since it reuses waste newspapers. The hammer mills used to grind up the newspapers use little energy and produce virtually no heat, as compared to fiberglass insulation. Cellulose insulation has an R-value of about R-3.6 per inch.

Cellulose is normally blown into the cavity of the wall being insulated, allowing it to fill all the small voids in the wall created by electrical and plumbing fixtures. The interior walls of the home are covered with a netting material used to hold the cellulose in place until the interior drywall is applied. Another advantage to cellulose insulation is that it can be installed in the walls of older homes by drilling holes in the walls, and blowing in the product. Cellulose must be applied at the density specified by manufacturer to avoid settling. If the insulation settles, voids will occur in the walls, and the energy efficiency of the building will suffer. Another approach to applying cellulose involves adding a binding agent to the insulation, and spraying the cellulose onto the wall cavities. The bonding agent allows the insulation to stick to the wall until it is covered with drywall. It is important that cellulose insulation be kept dry, because it will absorb more moisture than fiberglass insulation, losing most of its insulating properties. If cellulose insulation is allowed to become wet, it may take some time for it to dry.

These two insulating products, fiberglass and cellulose, are by far the most common products in use today. There are some other insulating fiber products available such as rock wool or vermiculite, but these products are not widely used in comparison with fiberglass or cellulose.

Foam Insulation

There are other forms of insulation available as options to standard fiberglass or cellulose, these consist of rigid foam panels and spray in place foams.

Expanded Polystyrene (EPS) foam insulation has many uses in home construction. EPS is made in the form of large pre-cast sheets or can be cast into specific shapes (ICFs), and it is an effective, relatively inexpensive, insulator (all foam insulators are more expensive than fiberglass). EPS foam is made primarily from petroleum, and has the environmental issues associated with petroleum. EPS is also very long lasting, and does not readily break down when placed in landfills.

EPS foam insulation is commonly used in masonry homes

If EPS is installed on the interior of a home, a fire resistant barrier such as drywall should be installed over the foam board.

EPS is used primarily as a sheet-insulating product for masonry walls or floors, normally being installed on the interior of the home. High-density EPS panels are available, and can be installed on

101

the exterior of basement walls.

EPS is used against masonry walls for a couple of reasons: first, it provides a descent insulation value of about R-3.7 per inch. EPS does not absorb water, which helps when it is placed directly against a masonry wall, as most masonry will transfer water through its structure. If you place materials that absorb water, against a masonry wall, you create a nice place for molds or mildew to grow, which can be very unhealthy for people.

As stated before, EPS is also used in the manufacture of insulated concrete forms, and to make ceiling insulation baffles. If you use blown-in insulation in your ceilings, you need to ensure that air can travel from under your soffits, along the roof, and out the upper roof vents. This natural convective airflow helps to keep your attic cool. Ceiling insulation baffles prevent the blown-in insulation from sealing against the roof, and provide a space for airflow.

Yet another type of insulation board is made from polyurethane or polyisocyanurate foams. These foams are made by a chemical reaction between poly-alcohol compounds and isocyanurates, and produce closed cell foam boards. This type foam boards are normally faced on both sides with an aluminum foil, which helps to reflect radiant energy from both the inside and outside of the home. Insulating sheathing boards are available in thicknesses ranging from 1/2" to 2" thick, and have an R-value ranging from R-4 to R-7 per inch of thickness. This product is used as a sheathing material with insulating properties on many buildings. Issues with this type of product are that they are made from petroleum compounds, and have the same potential environmental impact as other petroleum based materials. It should also be noted that rigid foam panels do not have the same shear strength of wood panels. In a frame home, the vertical studs provide the vertical support for the building, while the exterior sheathing provides most of the shear, or side to side, strength for the building. These two components work together to make a strong, stable building. When used as the exterior sheathing, a home with foam panels will not be as strong as a home with wooden panels in severe weather such as a tornado. These foam panels must also be covered with a fire resistant material such as drywall when used on the interior of a home.

Foam panel boards can be used as a sheathing material

102

Another type of foam insulation is sprayed in place on the walls of the home during construction.

Polyicynene foam is a sprayed in place foam insulation product. The polyicynene foam is mixed using special equipment at the job site, and applied directly to the walls or ceiling of the home. This foam expands rapidly, and fills any voids or cavities in the walls. Polyicynene foam is a combination of two petroleum-based chemicals, and produces carbon dioxide and a small amount of heat as it expands, and has the same environmental issues as any petroleum based compound. Polyicynene foam does not off-gas any chemicals into the home once installed, and does not support the growth of bacteria or fungi. This is especially important for people with allergies, asthma, or other respiratory problems, because polyicynene foam does not add contaminates to indoor air. Polyicynene is an effective insulator with an insulation value of about R-3.6 per inch, and since it expands to fill voids in the walls, it effectively controls air infiltration. Polyicynene foam is also effective at absorbing sound, which will help isolate your home from the outdoor environment. Because polyicynene foam is sprayed in place, it expands past the wall cavities; the excess foam must be shaved or cut off the wall before the wall can be covered with drywall. This process creates a moderate amount of foam waste, which must be disposed of. The foam waste can be shredded, and placed in the attic of the home as insulation rather than being sent to a landfill.

How much insulation do you need in your home? The amount of insulation you put in your home depends on the area in which you live, and how much you want to invest in the insulation of the home. Many building codes today require an insulation value of R-19 in all walls, and R-30 in the ceiling. It must be understood that these numbers are only average insulation values; some warmer climates will have much lower insulation requirements, while some colder climates may have higher insulation requirements. Be sure and check with your local building authorities for the requirements in your area. It should be noted that if you choose to add more insulation to your home than required by the local guidelines, your home would consume less energy on an annual basis than other homes in your area. As fuel prices continue to increase, you will save more money every year. It may only take a few years to recoup an investment in extra insulation, after which time you will be saving energy and money.

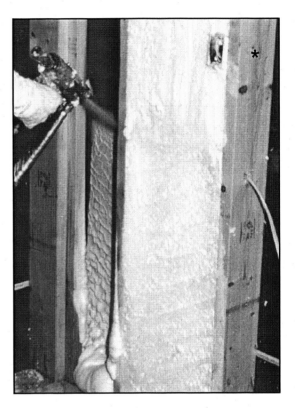

Polyicynene is a spray in place expanding foam insulation

Air Infiltration Barriers

Most insulating materials require two conditions to work effectively: first, air cannot be allowed to enter or pass through voids in the insulation material, secondly, water vapor from the interior of the home cannot be allowed to pass through the insulation material toward the outdoors.

Generally, the two major areas of heat loss in a home come from windows/doors, and through air infiltration. Air infiltration can siphon off as much as half of the heating or cooling energy used in a home.

An air infiltration barrier allows water vapor, but not air, to pass through its fabric

How does air infiltration occur? There are many sources of potential air infiltration in every home. Every time you open a door to exit or enter the house, you allow unconditioned air to rush into the home. A small crack between the window trim and the window can let air escape or enter. The hole where the electrical service enters your home can be another source of air infiltration. Actually, there are hundreds of possible entry points, in a standard home, through which air can pass, allowing conditioned air to escape and unconditioned air to enter.

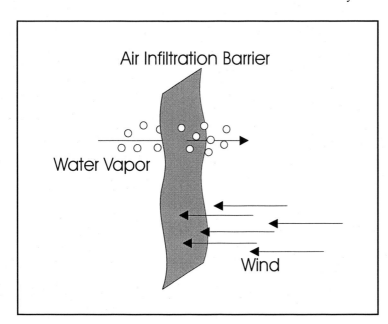

Air Infiltration Barrier

Water Vapor

Wind

The only way to slow down air infiltration is to carefully seal every possible entry point, and to design the home to reduce air transfer as we enter or leave the home.

There are a variety of ways to seal air entry points. The most common method of slowing down air infiltration is by using an air infiltration barrier, of which there are several different variations available. An air infiltration barrier is a fabric that eliminates the ability of the air to blow through openings and voids in the walls, if properly installed. The other important feature of air infiltration barrier is that it does allow any water vapor trapped inside the walls of the home to exit through the fabric. Air infiltration barriers restrict air movement, but allow the movement of water vapor through a wall. An air infiltration barrier is usually applied only to the exterior vertical walls of the home, before the exterior sheathing, but not the ceiling or floor. All of the seams of the air infiltration barrier are sealed with a special tape in order to provide a solid barrier.

An air infiltration barrier only restricts airflow in the exterior vertical walls. Areas such as the ceiling or floor require other measures to reduce air infiltration. These other sources of air infiltration can only be reduced with the use of a vapor barrier on the ceiling, and carefully sealing electrical boxes, electrical wires, plumbing pipes, or heating pipes coming up from the floor or down from the ceiling. Every place that a window, door, pipe, or wire enters the house or passes through an exterior wall, floor, or ceiling, a hole is created through which air can pass. You can use caulking and expanding foam sealants to seal these areas. Use caulking in areas that are visible such as around doors or windows, and expanding foams in areas that are not visible.

For fiberglass insulation, and other water absorbing insulators, to do their job well, they must be kept dry. An interior vapor barrier on modern homes performs this function. The vapor barrier is basically a sheet of plastic placed on all the interior walls and ceilings, beneath the drywall or other wall covering. We, the occupants of our homes, create a lot of water vapor on a daily basis, as we shower, do laundry, wash dishes, cook, and breath. All these actions, as well as others, create water vapor inside our homes. The average family releases between 3 and 6 gallons of water, in the form of water vapor, into the indoor air of the home on any given day. The more people who live in a home, the more water vapor will be released inside the home. The amount of water vapor inside the house is generally higher than the level of water vapor outside the house.

The air infiltration barrier is used to cover the exterior walls of the home

Water vapor wants to move from areas of higher concentration to areas of lower concentration. The vapor barrier prevents the water vapor inside the house from passing through the interior walls, and becoming trapped in the insulation. In cold climates, if the water vapor is allowed to move toward the outer wall of the house, the water will condense out of the air when the water vapor gets cold enough (the water vapor changes into liquid water). This happens the same way that water condenses on the sides of a glass filled with iced tea on a hot summer day. If the water vapor is allowed to pass through the wall, the water will usually condense at some point inside the insulation, where it will be absorbed by the insulation. Adding more insulation to the home will not prevent this process from occurring. At some point in the wall, the temperature will be at a level that will promote condensation.

If the insulation is allowed to get wet, it looses some or all of its insulating effectiveness. The house then has little or no insulation against the elements, and heat is readily transferred through the walls. Other side effects of wet insulation are the possibility of mold or mildew growing within the walls (a health hazard), or the possibility of damage to the sheathing products such as gypsum wallboard.

Vapor barriers prevent moisture in the home from passing through the exterior walls

The most important issue with a vapor barrier is how good of a job the crew does when installing it. Most builders will tack the vapor barrier to all interior walls and ceilings, which meets the building codes, but unfortunately ignores many areas where water vapor can escape the house. The most ignored areas are around the rim joist (where the floor system rests on the foundation, and supports the walls above), the floor itself, and the numerous penetrations in the walls for windows, doors, and mechanical systems. It is important to effectively seal all of these penetrations through the vapor barrier. This allows the vapor barrier to do its job and keep the water vapor in the home, not in the insulation. Another advantage of a well-sealed vapor barrier is that the vapor barrier can aid the air infiltration barrier in keeping air from moving through the walls of the home.

The most standard type of vapor barrier is clear plastic sheeting. Other types of vapor barriers consist of special gypsum wallboard; with a vapor proof membrane adhered on the backside of the sheathing. Special sealing tape is used at the seams and corners to provide a good vapor barrier seal for the home.

Problems with "Super Insulating"

Once you have sealed all the entry points for air infiltration, and you have highly insulated your home, you have created another set of problems. Such a home is considered to be "Super Insulated". A super insulated home does not allow much air infiltration, nor does it allow the transfer of much heat to the outdoor environment. The air is trapped inside the home.

Have you ever noticed how the air in a normal, slightly leaky home, can smell stale at times during the winter? The problem with trapping the air inside your home is that we, the occupants, release a lot of potentially harmful chemicals into the air of our homes. When we breathe, we take in oxygen and expel carbon dioxide. It is true that we only use a small portion of the oxygen in the air, but it is also true that we can tolerate only a small amount of carbon dioxide in the air we breathe. We also use many chemicals in our homes on a daily basis, and some of these chemicals can be harmful if not expelled from the air we breathe. Sources of these chemicals are everyday cooking, cleaning fluids, soaps, hair spray, nail polish, paints, etc. Take a few minutes to read the labels of the products you use everyday, you may be surprised by what is really in those bottles.

Another issue with trapping the air in your home is the collection of dust, dirt, and other debris, which enter and collect in our homes. We create all sorts of dust and dirt with our daily activities. We track things in from the outside world, pests and rodents, or our pets can bring in all sorts of things. There are microscopic organisms that live in all parts of our homes; dust mites are a prime example. Dust mites feed on the dead skin we slough off every day, and they emit waste or dander. This dander can irritate some people and cause allergic reactions in others.

Paper media filters are much more effective than standard HVAC filters

There are two solutions to the buildup of these substances in our homes; the first is the use of an air filtration system attached to your HVAC (heating, ventilation, air conditioning) system, the second option is to install an air-to-air heat recovery ventilator. You can even utilize both of these options at the same time.

As far as air filtration systems, there are many options. Most of these systems replace the small, inefficient filter that is normally installed on an HVAC system with a much more efficient filter. The original equipment filter installed on most furnace systems does very little to clean the air that passes through it, their main function is to capture large debris, and keep them from getting caught in the circulation fan or system ducts.

One filter option is an electronic filter, which charges dust particles with a static electrical charge, and then attracts them to a filter to be removed from the air. Usually, you clean the filter material by washing it in your dishwasher on a monthly basis. These filters do a relatively good job of cleaning the air, but are not the most effective filters available.

Another option is called a media filter. Media filters consist of a large piece of filter material, folded into an accordion shape, which allows it to fit into the air return duct. There are a variety of media types used in media filters, ranging from a specialized paper media to glass microfiber media. All of these media types have a very fine mesh, which allows the filter to remove the majority of pollen, mold, dust, grease, soot, and smoke. The media can remove things from the air as small as .01 microns in diameter. A micron is equal to .000039 inches. Media filters need to be changed about every 6 months.

There is a limit to what any filter can do for the air quality in your home. These filters can remove most of the dirt and dust from the air inside your home, but are not effective at removing the chemicals, carbon dioxide, or bad smells. At some point the air in your home needs to be changed, or exchanged with clean air from the outdoors.

Heat transferred to fresh air

Stale indoor air to be exhausted

Fresh outdoor air to come indoors

A heat recovery ventilator can remove stale air from your home

An air-to-air heat recovery ventilator is a special device, which attaches to your HVAC system, and brings fresh air into your home and expels older, stale air. The key thing that a heat recovery ventilator does is retain a good portion of the conditioning of the air (heating or cooling) from the out going stale air, and transfer that conditioning to the fresh air being brought into the home. Some manufacturers claim to capture 80% of the conditioning energy from the out going air.

Heat recovery ventilators will add about $1500 to the cost of your home. This cost may cause you to ask the question, "If I insulate my home well and then need to spend an extra $1500 to clean the air, what is the point?" The point is that you reduce your energy consumption, which helps protect the environment, and you provide your family with healthier air to breath inside your home. Unfortunately, we sometimes have to spend some extra money in order to take advantage of what new technologies have to offer.

Windows and Doors

All homes have windows and doors. It is important that you purchase quality windows and doors for your home, because it does not do much good if you insulate and seal the shell of your home, only to install cheap windows and doors, which leak air, have little or no insulation value, and negate your other insulating efforts.

Doors are important because we use them everyday, many times per day. Any exterior door should have an insulated core, and good weather stripping in order to provide a good seal. Insulated exterior doors are made with a variety of materials; most are made of steel or fiberglass. Most wooden exterior doors are solid core (solid wood), and have only the insulation value inherent to wood. Steel and fiberglass doors have a core insulating material of fiberglass or foam, greatly increase the insulation value of the door. The R-value of wood is about R-1 per inch, while the R-value of fiberglass or foam ranges from R-3.2 to R-7 per inch. It is important to the energy efficiency of your home that your exterior doors be as efficient as possible. Doors can be manufactured to resemble wood, but most will unfortunately not have the beauty and luster of real wood. There are some high-end exterior doors available that are made of steel or fiberglass, and have a wood veneer adhered to the outside. These doors can be finished to obtain the beauty of real wood, while retaining the insulation properties of other materials. It is important to note that real wood, exposed to the elements, will periodically need to be refinished.

A quality entry door will make your home more energy efficient

All doors need to have effective weather stripping. Weather stripping is the plastic or rubber seal around all the edges of a door. Weather stripping is important because it is designed to reduce air infiltration past the door. If the weather stripping does not seal well, you will be letting air into or out of your home continuously, reducing your energy efficiency.

There are two other things you can do to your exterior doors to make them more energy efficient. The first is to add a good quality storm door to the outside of the exterior door. A storm door will offer you a few benefits. It improves the energy efficiency of the exterior door by trapping the air between the two doors. This trapped air acts as a buffer between your indoor environment and the outdoor environment, slowing down the heat transfer rate between the two. A storm door can also add another level of security to your home, because most storm doors have locking mechanisms. This is a good feature if you want to leave the exterior door open on nice days, and still be able to keep people from entering the home. Lastly, many storm doors have screens incorporated into them, allowing for some ventilation of the home during periods of moderate weather.

The second way to increase the energy efficiency of your exterior doors is to design an air-lock or vestibule inside the doorway. An air-lock is a small space, or room, inside your exterior doorway, with another door that opens into the living space. This second door also has weather stripping like the exterior door. This air-lock serves two purposes. First, it acts as a buffer between the indoors and the outdoors, reducing the rate of heat transfer. Secondly, if the air-lock is large enough for you to stand inside, allowing you to close the exterior door before you open the interior air-lock door, you prevent large amounts of very cold air from rushing in when you enter your home.

An entry door air-lock will help reduce energy losses

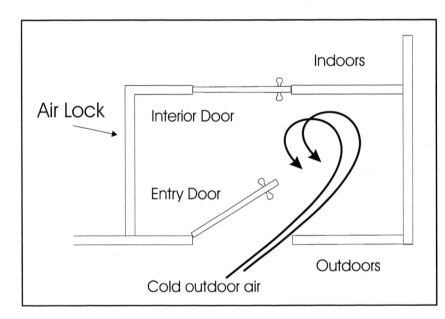

Stopping this inflow of cold air can make a large difference in the energy efficiency of your home. A laundry room between the garage and the living area can serve as an air-lock between the common entrance to your home and the garage or outdoors.

Energy efficient windows are very important if you want to build an energy efficient house. We lose large amounts of energy through windows, because glass has very little insulation value. Do you know how cold a window feels on a winter day? This is because the window is allowing heat loss. Windows loose heat in four basic ways; by conduction, heat being transmitted through the glass, by convection, warm air circulating past a cold window, and losing its heat, by radiation, the movement of infrared energy through the glass, and lastly, by air leaking past the seals in the moving parts of the window, and past improperly sealed window frames.

Window technology has drastically changed in the past 40 years. The old, single pane windows used in our parents homes, were terribly inefficient. Today we have high technology, multi-pane windows, with inert gasses between the panes, high tech coatings on the windowpanes, and efficient seals around the windows. All of these features combine to make windows much more efficient than in the past. This is not saying that we still do not lose a lot of energy through our windows; this just makes it possible to have windows in our homes without totally sacrificing energy efficiency.

One of the most important innovations in window technology has been the addition of metallic oxide coatings to the inside of multi-pane windows. These coatings are generally called low-E, or low emissivity coatings. These coatings are very thin, and almost transparent to the human eye. They are however, not transparent to all types of light energy.

Only a fraction of the light from the sun is visible to the human eye. Visible light is made of short wavelength light waves. Light waves with a still shorter wavelength are ultraviolet, or UV light waves. UV is the light that gives you a sunburn, ages your skin, and can fade or damage floors, carpeting, and upholstery in your home. Above the visible light spectrum are infrared light waves. Infrared light has a longer wavelength than visible light, and is felt as heat. The sun warms the earth with infrared radiation or light.

Standard low-E coatings allow the majority of the visible light to pass through the window, while reflecting most of the UV and Infrared light. What this means is that in the summer, in a climate where air conditioning is used, the visible light is allowed through the window while the majority of the infrared, or heat energy, is reflected back to the outdoors. This means that you have a much lower heat gain through the windows in your home, reducing your air conditioning costs. In a cold weather climate, a portion of the heat energy inside your home is reflected back into your home by the low-E coatings, again reducing your energy costs.

It needs to be understood that if you plan on taking advantage of the radiant energy from the sun to heat your home (passive solar heating), you must select your windows very carefully. If you use standard low-E coated windows on the south side of your home where the sun comes in, the low-E coating will block most of the solar heat energy that you want to capture. There are special low-e coatings available that allow for a higher rate of solar heat gain, an amount of solar gain almost equal to un-

Windows loose heat in a variety of ways

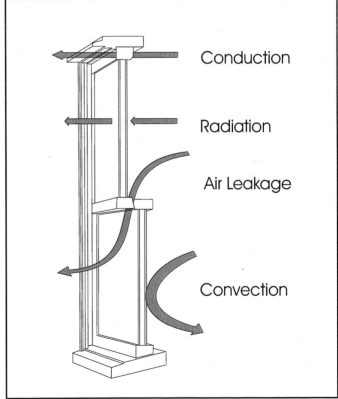

Conduction

Radiation

Air Leakage

Convection

coated, double pane windows. This type of window will give you the best balance between visible light transmittance, solar heat gain, and a low-e coating to help retain the heat inside your home. Your window supplier will be able to advise you on your window selections if you intend to utilize passive solar heating.

Casement windows are more energy efficient than double hung windows

Other issues with windows deal with how well the window seals against the window jamb, and the energy efficiency of the window frame. Today, most windows have good quality seals. Casement, or hinged windows allow less air leakage than double hung windows (windows which move up and down, past each other). Casement windows are more efficient because their locking mechanisms clamp the window tightly against the frame, reducing possible areas of air leakage. Double hung window seals cannot be sealed as tightly, because the windows must be able to slide past one another.

Window frame materials can also greatly affect the energy efficiency of the window unit. Some inexpensive windows are available with solid aluminum frames. Aluminum is a good conductor of heat, and thus makes these windows inefficient. More expensive, better quality window frames are made of a combination of materials, or incorporate a thermal break between the inside and the outside of the window frame. Combining materials to make a window frame is very popular. One of the best combinations is a wooden frame covered or clad with painted aluminum on the outside. This combination allows the home owner to have the best of both worlds, the beauty of wood inside the home, the thermal characteristics of wood, and a no maintenance painted aluminum finish on the outside of the window. This may also be the most expensive combination. Other combinations of window frame materials include wood with vinyl cladding, wood fiber frame with vinyl cladding, or a wood fiber frame with aluminum cladding.

You can also increase the energy efficiency of all of your windows by installing insulated blinds or window shades inside your home. These can be opened to allow light into your home during the daytime but can be closed to help your home retain heat during the night. These again can have a large impact on your energy consumption.

Other Options

There are still more things you can do to your home to reduce energy consumption. About one third of unwanted heat energy absorbed by your home comes from your roof, and through your ceiling. One thing that can have a major impact on the energy consumption of your home is ventilation. There are two ways you can use ventilation in your home to reduce heat gain.

The first is to ventilate the living areas of your home. Most people already do this on moderate days when they open the windows, and allow the air to pass through the home. There are a couple of ways in which this process can be improved. You can design the home to allow for effective cross ventilation (allowing the air to pass through the home unimpaired by doors or walls). This type of design will allow you to take advantage of a cool breeze. Another option is to use a large fan to pull air through the home, creating an artificial breeze. It is much less expensive to run a fan than it is to run an air conditioner. These fans are typically mounted in the ceiling, have a louvered face, and a switch for tuning the fan on or off. This type of "attic fan" was very common 40 years ago, but not so common today. Problems with this type of fan were

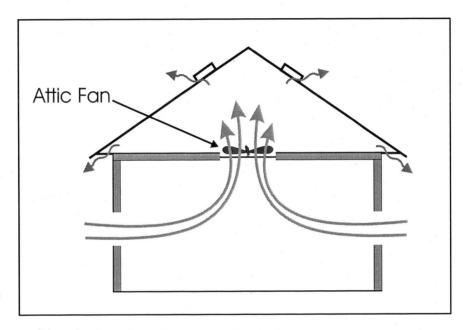

that they were noisy and had no insulation value, allowing heat loss in the winter. Today, there are smaller, less noisy attic fans with insulated doors. These fans are less obtrusive, are more energy efficient than their predecessors, and can help to keep your home cool on marginal days.

An attic fan can pull cool outdoor air through the home, cooling the living area and the attic

Another area for improving ventilation is your attic. Attics become very hot in the summer, as hot as 150 degrees Fahrenheit. This heat can slowly transfer the living areas of your home. If you can reduce the heat in your attic, you can reduce the heat being absorbed by your living spaces. This can be accomplished in a couple ways. First, you need adequate ventilation in the attic. All local building codes require a certain amount of ventilation in the roof structure and attic, but you can further reduce the heat in the attic by installing extra ventilation. With good vents, as the heat builds in the attic, the hot air will exit the upper vents (heat rises), and cooler air will be drawn into the lower vents creating a convective cycle. This occurs without any assistance, but may not be able to move the hot air out of the attic quickly enough. You can supplement this cycle by adding a powered roof vent to your home. This is a vent with fan and a built in thermostat. When the temperature in the attic gets hot enough, the fan turns on, and draws out the hot air; again, a fan is much less expensive to run than the air conditioner. This type of vent is also available with solar panels to provide energy for the fan. The attic can only get hot if the sun is shinning, and the fan only runs if the attic is hot.

Another option is to install a radiant barrier just below the roof of your home. A radiant barrier is a reflective material (aluminum foil), adhered to a paper backing. This is applied to the underside of the roofing rafters. This radiant barrier can reflect as much as 25% of the heat energy absorbed by your roof, back out through the roof. Over time, this can add up to a large amount of energy not absorbed by your home, and lower energy bills.

A radiant barrier in your attic can reduce your energy usage

There is still another product available for the interior of your home. Paint with a radiant energy reflective material included. This type of paint is not very common today, because it is a very new technology. The idea of this

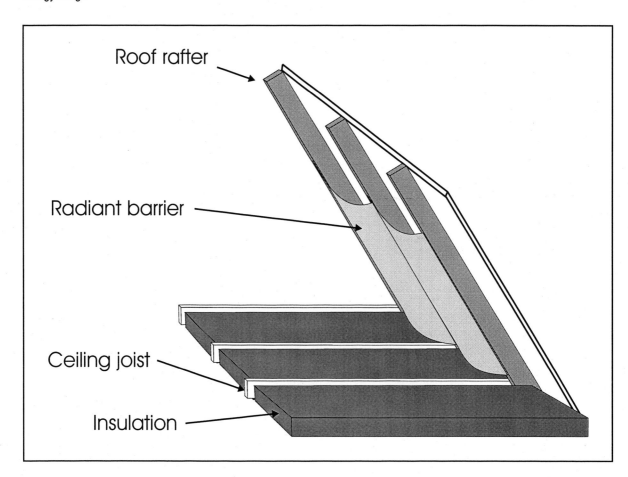

Roof rafter

Radiant barrier

Ceiling joist

Insulation

product is when it is applied to the interior surfaces of your home; it acts as a radiant barrier, reflecting radiant energy back into your home. Sounds too simple to work, but it does. The paint looks and acts like any other paint except it helps your home conserve energy. The benefit from this product is small in comparison to some others discussed previously, but every little bit of energy savings adds up to an overall large energy savings.

All of these things will add to the overall efficiency, comfort, healthiness of your home. There is a balance that must be maintained to keep your home livable and healthy. More information on this subject can be found at www.futurehomestoday.com.

6   Passive Solar Design

Solar design is designing a home to take advantage the heat energy available from the sun. The sun heats the earth everyday. In winter, the sun is heating the earth, but the angle at which the suns rays strike the earth are less direct and less effective. No matter what part of the country you live in, there is solar energy available, of which you can take advantage. If we design our homes to take advantage of the suns energy in the winter, we can reduce the amount of heat we need our furnace to produce in order to make us comfortable. If we reduce the amount of heat produced by the furnace, we reduce the amount of energy we use in our homes. As energy costs continue to increase, the financial returns of solar design will increase. In cold climates, it is possible to get as much as half of the heat for our homes from the sun without radically changing our homes or how we live. If every new house built took advantage of solar design, the amount of energy consumed for heating in this country would be drastically reduced. This chapter is designed to relay the general principles of passive solar heating; it will not cover the topics of calculating the heat loss of your home, or the available heat energy in your area. These topics are thoroughly covered in books dedicated entirely to solar heating, some of which are listed in the appendix.

Passive vs. Active Solar Heating

There are two general methods of solar heating available to homebuilders. These two methods are passive solar heating systems and active solar heating systems (there are many different variations of these two methods). Passive solar design involves building your home so that you can take advantage of the energy provided by the sun in the winter, allow that energy to enter your home, and store some of that energy for use after the sun sets. Passive solar heating does not involve the use of any moving parts, mechanical devices, sensors, or controls in order to capture and store the heat energy from the sun. Active solar design uses a mechanical system to capture, transfer, and store the suns energy for use in the home. These mechanical systems require a much larger initial investment to install

You can utilize free energy from the sun to help heat your home in the winter

the solar heating system. There is also the need for periodic maintenance of the mechanical systems used in an active solar heating system. Most active solar heating systems include items such as collector panels outside the home, heat transport pipes, heat storage tanks, pumps, electronics, and controls.

Active solar heating methods can also potentially fail, and cause damage to the home. (flooding from water loss, etc.) From a simplicity and overall adaptability standpoint, we will only discuss passive solar design in this chapter. It should be noted that active solar design has the potential to capture and store more of the suns energy than passive solar designs.

What are the disadvantages to building a passive solar home? None! Building to take advantage of passive solar potential merely means designing your home to take advantage of what solar energy is available in your climate. In order to take advantage of solar energy, we need to design the home to allow the suns energy to enter the home in the winter, and to be able to store some of that energy for later use. This can be accomplished by redistributing, or rearranging, some of the building materials used in construction of the home. The main construction materials that will need to be redistributed are concrete and windows. We use concrete for foundations, floors, or walls in almost every home constructed. We use windows to allow us to see out of our homes, and to let light into our homes. By changing the basic design model, moving some of these building components around, and orienting the home to the sun, we can take advantage of the heat energy the sun has to offer. A highly insulated home will increase the efficiency of solar design. The better insulated the home, the less heat energy is required to make the home comfortable during cold weather, the more effective the solar heating system.

Solar homes today do not require unsightly solar panels on the roof

Will your home look ugly or weird? No, not if it is well designed. A solar heated home does not have to look like it belongs on another planet, or look like the solar system was an after thought. If designed properly, you should not even know that the home uses passive solar heating. Solar design has changed quite a bit since its heydays in the 1970's. Today, solar heated homes are designed to look very similar to the average home. The most visible features of a solar home will be its orientation to the south, and the windows located on the southern side of the home. These are the windows that allow the sunshine into your home. Will your home get too hot on a sunny day? No, not if it is well designed. Too many windows should not be placed on the south side of the home. This is called "over glazing", and causes some solar homes to get too hot during the day. Will your home feel too cold? No, not if it is well designed. Passive solar heating is designed to augment the heating system of the home, reducing energy usage. Good design is essential to any home, and more so in a passively solar heated home.

Passive Solar Basics

The basic idea of passive solar design is to: first, allow sunshine to enter your home through windows, second, allow the suns energy to heat massive, heavy objects in the home in order to store the heat (concrete floors or walls), and third, allow this stored heat energy to transfer to the air inside the home when the sun is not shining (night time). This is a simplistic description of passive solar design, but it conveys the general concept.

Stand in front of a window on a sunny, cold winter day, and you immediately feel the rays of the sun start to warm your body. Your body is absorbing the suns heat. The energy from the sun is made up of three general types of light energy. There is visible light, which is the part of the light spectrum we are able to see with our eyes. Visible light also allows us to see the light reflected by the objects around us, creating the colors that we see. There is infrared light, which is the part of the light spectrum that we cannot see, but we do feel. Infrared light energy is the warmth we feel when we are standing in the sunshine. Lastly, there is ultraviolet light, which is another portion of the light spectrum that we

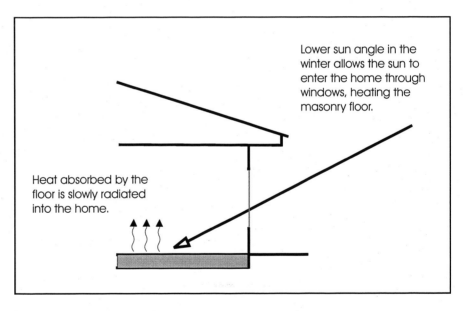

Lower sun angle in the winter allows the sun to enter the home through windows, heating the masonry floor.

Heat absorbed by the floor is slowly radiated into the home.

cannot see. Ultraviolet light energy can give you a sunburn when you spend too much time in the sunshine without protection. Ultraviolet light will also fade the colors of flooring and upholstery. The infrared light is the light in which we are interested, because it transfers the suns energy through the windows, and into your home in a passive solar home design.

Infrared light energy from the sun does not directly heat the air in your home; it heats the objects it strikes. Because of this infrared energy, when you stand in front of the window, you feel the warmth on your body, but the air temperature

119

around you is not directly changed. This is the reason why a solar mass is needed in a passive solar heated home. We need a massive substance (solar mass) built into the home for the suns rays to shine upon, and absorb the suns energy. The solar mass absorbs the infrared heat from the sun, and then allows the absorbed heat to be transferred to the air in your house. This indirect heating of the air in the home occurs via convection.

Sun Energy

The sun is always shining. On clear days, a large portion of the suns heat energy is allowed to reach the surface of the earth. The atmosphere of the earth acts as a filter for the suns energy, absorbing some and reflecting some. Only a portion of the suns heat energy still reaches the earth on cloudy days. The angle at which the suns rays strike any point of the earth changes during the year. We will only discuss how the suns energy affects the land areas in the northern hemisphere of the earth, such as the United States. The weather in the northern hemisphere is opposite of that in the southern hemisphere at any point during the year. June in the United States is summer, while June in Australia is winter. The suns rays strike the northern hemisphere more directly in the summer months, and less directly in the winter months. The suns rays strike the northern hemisphere the most directly at the summer solstice, or on June 21st. On June 21st, the sun will be visible for more hours than on any other day of the year. With more sunshine, there is more energy to

The angle between the sun and the earth changes during the year

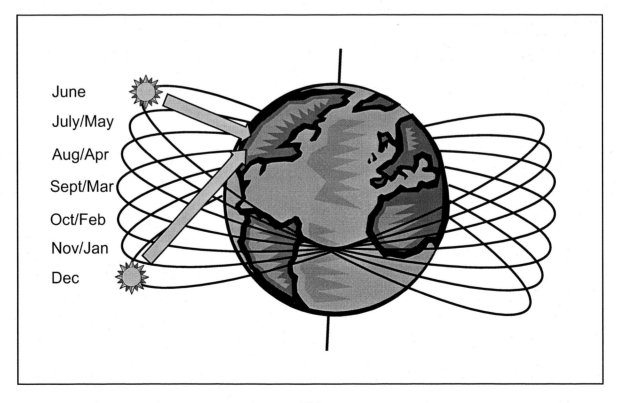

June

July/May

Aug/Apr

Sept/Mar

Oct/Feb

Nov/Jan

Dec

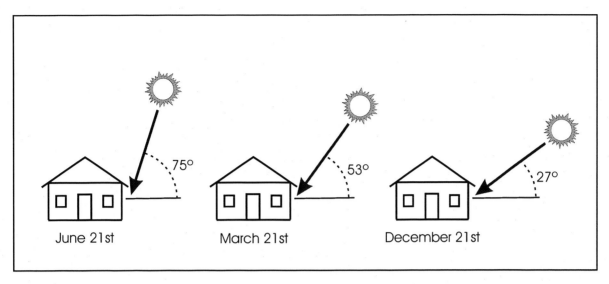

June 21st   March 21st   December 21st

The sun angle is greater in the summer and less in the winter (the sun angle varies depending on the latitude of your location)

be absorbed by the earth, resulting in higher temperatures. The suns rays strike the northern hemisphere less directly at the winter solstice, or on December 21st. On December 21st the sun will be visible for fewer hours than on any other day of the year. Less sunshine, less energy to be absorbed by the earth, resulting in lower temperatures. In between these dates the suns angle slowly changes from one extreme to the other, passing through spring and fall. This holds true for all parts of the United States. The further south you are, the more heat energy is available in the winter, while the further north you are, the less heat energy will be available in the winter.

Good passive solar design will absorb the heat energy available in the winter, and resist the absorption of heat energy in the summer. Orientation of the home to the sun is very important to the livability, and the creation of comfort in your home.

In the summer, the sun rises in the northeast, travels along a high arc across the sky, and sets in the northwest. The sun may be visible for 14 hours or more in the middle of the summer. The suns rays are more perpendicular to the earth in the summer, allowing more of the suns energy to be absorbed by the earth, making the weather hotter during the summer. During the summer, your shadow at noon will be short because the sun is almost directly overhead, and shade can only be found directly under an object or overhang.

During the winter months the sun rises in the southeast. It then takes a long, low arching path across the sky, and sets in the southwest. The sun may only shine for about 9 hours during a winter day. The sun is much lower in the sky, and its rays are much less effective, because of the angle at which they strike the earth in the northern hemisphere. The sun is producing as much heat as during the summer, but all of the heat energy does not reach the United States because of the sun angle, creating the colder climate of winter. Your shadow at

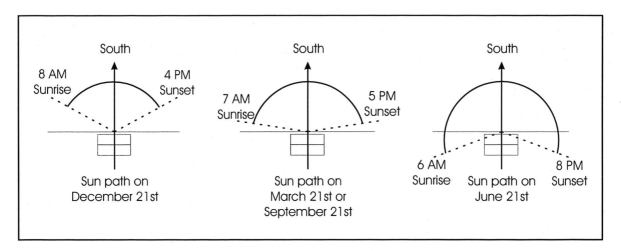

| Sun path on December 21st | Sun path on March 21st or September 21st | Sun path on June 21st |

The locations of sunrise and sunset also change during the year (the sun angle varies depending on the latitude of your location)

noon in the winter will always be long, because of the relationship between our location on the earth and the sun.

The low angle of the sun in the winter allows the sunshine to penetrate your home through south facing windows. This sunshine can be used to help heat your home if it is properly designed. This south facing side of the home can be called the "solar side" of the house.

Having the living areas of your home facing the south can dramatically effect the interior environment. Having sunshine penetrating your home on a cold winter day can greatly improve your mindset, and your attitude. You can feel comfortable and warm sitting in the sunshine when the temperature outside is well below freezing.

Orientation

In order to allow the winter sunshine into your home, the solar side of your home needs to face the direction from which the sunshine is coming, or south.

In the winter the sun makes a long, low arch across the sky, reaching its highest point due south from your home. During the winter, the most heat energy for solar heating will be available between the hours of 10AM and 2PM. There is heat energy available from 8AM to 10AM, and from 2PM to 4PM, but it is much less effective than during the 10 to 2 time frame.

During these less effective hours, the sun is lower on the horizon, and at a greater angle to the windows of the solar side of your home. When the sun is low on the horizon, the light has to pass through more of the earth's atmosphere before it reaches your home. The atmosphere absorbs or reflects much of the suns energy, preventing it from reaching your location on the earth. As the sun rises in the east (8AM), it is also at a much greater angle to the windows of your solar side than later in the morning (10AM). This angle also prevents some of the suns energy from entering the home, because the windows reflect some of that energy. This is also the case from 2PM to 4PM as the sun sets. These are the reasons why the 10AM to 2PM time frame is the most effective for solar heating.

You will have the best potential for solar gain if you face the solar side of your home due south. The farther from due south you orient your home, the less solar energy will be available for you to capture on the solar side of your home.

A house facing due south will be able to take full advantage of the suns energy, or allow you to realize 100% of the available sun energy. If you face your home 22.5° off of due south, you will only be able to realize or capture about 92% of the available sun energy. This holds true if you orient the home 22.5° to the east or west. Because the windows used to capture the solar energy will be at an angle to the sun rays when it reaches it's highest and most effective point, the sunshine does not directly enter the house during the most efficient heating hours (10AM to 2PM). You lose some the available sun energy, because it is reflected off the windows, which are at more of an angle to the sun.

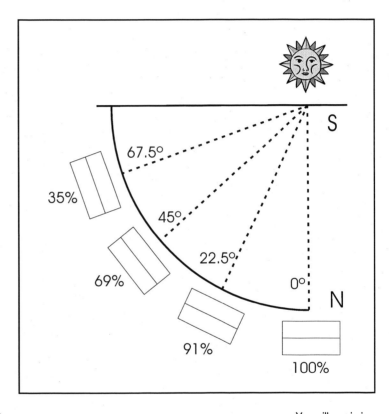

If you set your home at a 45° degree angle to due south, you will only be able to realize about 70% of the available sun energy with the solar side of your home. This pattern continues as you change the orientation of your home. The further from due south you orient your home. The less sun energy will be available to the solar side of your home. It is important to understand that as the heat energy available to one side of your home decreases, the heat energy available to another side of the home will increase.

You will maximize the solar heating efficiency if you orient your home due south

Proper orientation can greatly improve the livability of your home. Before you build or design a home, investigate how orientation will affect your home in the area where you plan to live.

Windows

Determining the number of south facing windows designed into a passive solar heated home should be done with care. Depending on the area in which you live, the heat available from the sun can be overwhelming on a bright, sunny day. If the home is designed with too many south facing windows, too much of the solar heat will be allowed to buildup inside the home, making it uncomfortable. This is called "over glazing". When the sun shines, the temperature in the home rises, and you are forced to vent excess heat to the outdoors, which is not an efficient solar heating scenario. A properly designed passive solar home will not have these problems; the captured heat will be absorbed by the solar mass, and will slowly radiate into the home.

The types of windows used in a solar heated home are important

Window selection in a passive solar home is very important, because there are many different types windows available today. The most efficient windows available today are called low-E, or low-emissivity windows. Standard low-e windows have a coating of a metallic oxide on the interior side of the glass that filters out or reflects most of the ultraviolet and infrared rays from the sun, keeping them from entering the home, while allowing a majority of the visible light into the home. Infrared light provides the bulk of available heat for solar heating. If your windows do not allow the infrared light to enter the home, they do not allow much of the solar heat energy to enter the home. There are special low-e coated windows available that allow for high solar heat gain as opposed to standard low-e windows. These windows allow for almost as much solar heat gain as uncoated, double glazed windows. Low-E windows also keep some heat inside the home from radiating to the outdoors. This is good, because it helps to make the windows more efficient, loosing less heat energy. Standard low-E windows are great for the east, west, or north windows in your home. On these sides of the home, this type of window will help to conserve energy, while allowing light into the home. Low-E windows placed on the west side of the home will also reduce the amount of heat absorbed from the sun as it sets in the west during the summer months.

For the south side of your home, the solar side, you will want to use windows with a high solar heat gain low-e coating. This type of window will allow the majority of the suns heat energy to enter the home, while still offering the other advantages of a low-e coated window, high visible light transmittance and good energy retention characteristics.

All windows allow for the loss of large amounts of heat to the outdoors, because no window provides good insulation value. To increase the thermal efficiency of windows you can add a window insulation system. These systems are simply a material with some insulating value placed over, or in front of the window to reduce heat loss when the sun is not shining. These systems are almost always used indoors.

Insulated window curtains are the simplest form of window insulation. A well made insulating curtain can double the thermal efficiency of any window. During the day when the sun is shinning the curtains are opened to allow light and heat to enter the home. After the sun sets, the curtains can be closed to conserve heat, and provide privacy. Insulating curtains must be made to have very little clearance between the curtain and the wall, floor, and ceiling. The larger the clearance, the more air is allowed to circulate behind the curtain, reducing thermal efficiency. A valance at the top of the curtain can be used to reduce airflow over the top of the curtain. Attaching the sides of the curtain to the wall create an effective seal, and the bottom can be sealed by making the clearance of the curtain close to the floor. Curtains can be made with several layers of material, or even with a thin insulating material incorporated into them.

Un-insulated windows loose large amounts of energy

Another type of window insulation system involves insulated panels. These panels can be made of foam board, covered with fabric or a wood veneer. These panels can be made to store in pockets adjacent to the window, or to fold up and out of the way like a bi-fold closet door. A well-sealed panel insulation system will offer even better energy efficiency than any curtain. The only drawback to this type of system is that they are difficult or expensive to make, and they may be inconvenient to store when not in use.

Selecting the proper windows for your solar home to help capture the solar energy, while providing a form of insulation such as curtains to help retain that energy, will make your home more efficient.

The Solar Mass

What is a solar mass, and why do I need one? The solar mass is a massive, heavy object placed inside the home, and is used to collect and store the heat energy from the sun. The solar mass also acts as temperature buffer for the living area. While the sun is shinning on the solar mass, the infrared heat is being absorbed for later use. If the solar mass temperature is less than the interior air temperature desired by the occupants of the home, most of the suns heat energy will be absorbed by the solar mass. This heat is transferred and equalized within the solar mass by means of conduction. Even while the sun is heating the solar mass, heat is being transferred into the house. This heat transfer occurs in two ways: first, by radiation of heat energy from the solar mass to solid objects in the home, and secondly, by convection as air moves past the warm solar mass, and heat is transferred to the air in the home. After the sun has set and the house is no longer collecting heat energy, the interior air temperature will begin to fall. As this happens, excess heat from the solar mass will be transferred to the interior of the home as the stored heat energy seeks equilibrium between the living area temperature, and that of the solar mass. When the sun is not shinning (night or cloudy day), the solar mass will continue to release any stored heat into the home. This occurs until the solar mass, and the interior of the home reach equal temperatures.

Concrete can be formed to provide the structure of the home while acting as the solar mass

Of what should the solar mass for your home be made? All heavy materials will absorb, and hold the solar energy. The common choices for a solar mass are various types of masonry, or liquids such as water. Different substances absorb and store the suns heat energy with different efficiencies. Masonry is not a particularly efficient storage medium for absorbing and storing heat, but it just happens to be a substance we typically use in the construction of a home (foundation, basement walls, or slab floor).

Water is about twice as efficient as masonry at storing heat. The only problem with water is that it can be inconvenient to store or utilize in the living area of the home where you need the heat. Would a leak from a 1000 gallon water tank in your living room be a problem? If the heated water is stored in a remote of the home, it may also require the use of mechanical means to transport it from the solar collector, to the point of storage, and to the living area where the heat is needed. There are liquids that are even more efficient than water at storing heat. These liquids have additional disadvantages such as cost, or corrosiveness. Masonry does not have these particular problems.

Some of the inefficiencies of heat in a masonry mass can be overcome, within limits, by adding more mass to the interior of the home. The more mass in the area heated by the sun, the more heat storage capacity the solar mass will have. Additional mass can be accomplished by placing a masonry wall or planter in the area of sunshine, or by increasing the thickness or size of the solar mass.

The solar mass needs to be thermally isolated (insulated) from the ground below. The mean temperature of the ground below your home (about 58° F) is lower than the temperature you want in your home, or in your solar mass. Insulation will help to keep the heat absorbed by your solar mass from transferring to the ground, and being lost.

There are many different designs of passive solar heating. These range from simple designs where the solar mass is the floor of the home, to elaborate designs where the solar mass has ducts or air pathways through which heated air can flow via natural convection, or with mechanical assistance. These different designs will all perform their designed function, just with different efficiencies.

House layout

How should a passive solar heated house be arranged to be the most effective and comfortable? In non-solar houses, you can place or arrange the rooms in whatever manner suits the family, and the building site. This is because the heat for the building is supplied by a mechanical device, and distributed evenly through the house. In a passive solar heated home, the arrangement of the rooms is a bit more important.

Since a good part of the heat for the home will be provided by the sun, and mainly in the rooms facing to the

The layout of the home is important in maximizing solar gain

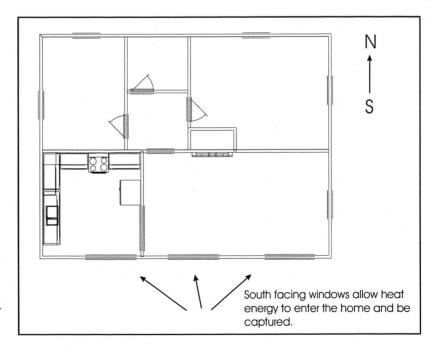

South facing windows allow heat energy to enter the home and be captured.

127

south, it is important to arrange the home to work with this heating system. This is important for the comfort level of the home, even though most solar heated homes will have a mechanical heating system to supplement the solar heating system. This supplemental heating system is needed for a couple of reasons. First, the sun does not always shine on a daily basis. If a winter storm system in your area, you may not see the sun for several days. During these times, you will need a supplemental heating system to make your home comfortable. Secondly, it will probably be the case that your solar heating system will only provide a portion of your heating needs. This will vary depending on the efficiency of your solar heating system, the thermal efficiency of your home, where you live, and so forth. For any number of these reasons you may need to continuously use a supplemental heating system to make your home comfortable.

Glass on the south facing side of the home allows for the capture of solar energy

The rooms of the home facing south will receive the benefit of the suns heat energy. These rooms will require windows large enough to enable the suns heat to enter the home and be captured. Because of these factors, the rooms that face south should be the public areas of the home, such as the living room, family room, and kitchen. Again the sun will provide the majority of the heat needed when it is shining, and the supplemental heating system will provide the heat otherwise.

Rooms that will not be continuously occupied, and thus require less heat during part of the day, can be located on the north side of the home away from the main source of heat. These rooms include closets, laundry room, bathrooms, and even bedrooms. All of these rooms can also utilize supplemental heat to make them comfortable when occupied. In the case of these rooms, the supplemental heat can be in the form of a whole house heating system with heating zones, or small, localized heaters. These small localized heaters might prove to be more efficient than the whole house system, depending upon their efficiency, and how they are used.

All of these ideas lead to the general shape of a passive solar heated home as a rectangle, with a long side of a rectangle facing south, functioning as the solar side of the home, so that there is more surface area with which to capture the suns heat energy. The shape of a rectangle also keeps the rooms on the north side of the building from being located too far from the available solar heat. A square shaped house does not lend itself quite as well to passive solar heating, but will work. You may find that a square shaped house will have some rooms located too far from the solar heat source, and thus too cold to be comfortable. You may be able to solve some of these issues with supplemental heat. A rectangular shaped house, with a short side acting as the solar side, is too inefficient to be practical.

Location

Depending upon your location in the country, there are varying amounts of sun energy available for you to capture. In general, these things are the available solar energy at your latitude (how far you are north of the equator of the earth), and the average weather conditions in your part of the country. Typically, the further south you are located, the more sun energy will be available for your use, because the sun at its highest point in the winter sky is at a greater angle to the earth, the further south you go toward the equator.

Your location determines the viability of solar heating

Mean percentage of possible sunshine for selected cities.

	Jan	Feb	Mar	Apr	May	Jun	Jul	Aug	Sep	Oct	Nov	Dec	Average
Boise, Idaho	40	48	59	67	68	75	89	86	81	66	46	37	64
Chicago, Illinois	44	49	5	56	63	69	73	70	65	61	47	41	54
Denver, Colorado	67	67	65	63	61	69	68	68	71	71	67	65	67
Kansas City, Missouri	55	57	59	60	64	70	76	73	70	67	59	52	64
Minneapolis, Minnesota	49	54	55	57	67	64	72	69	60	54	40	40	57
Memphis, Tennessee	44	51	57	64	68	74	73	74	70	69	58	45	62
Oklahoma City, Oklahoma	57	60	63	64	65	74	75	78	74	68	64	57	67
Pittsburgh, Pennsylvania	32	38	45	50	57	62	64	61	62	54	39	30	50
Raleigh, North Carolina	50	56	59	64	67	65	62	62	63	64	62	52	61

Average Monthly Degree Days for selected cities.

	Jan	Feb	Mar	Apr	May	Jun	Jul	Aug	Sep	Oct	Nov	Dec	Total
Boise, Idaho	0	0	132	415	792	1017	1113	854	722	438	245	81	5809
Chicago, Illinois	0	0	66	279	705	1051	1150	1000	868	489	226	48	5882
Denver, Colorado	0	0	90	366	714	905	1004	851	800	492	254	48	5524
Kansas City, Missouri	0	0	39	220	612	905	1032	818	682	294	109	0	4711
Minneapolis, Minnesota	22	31	189	505	1014	1454	1631	1380	1166	621	288	81	8382
Memphis, Tennessee	0	0	18	130	447	698	729	585	456	147	22	0	3232
Oklahoma City, Oklahoma	0	0	15	164	498	766	868	664	527	189	34	0	3725
Pittsburgh, Pennsylvania	0	0	60	291	615	930	983	885	763	390	124	12	5053
Raleigh, North Carolina	0	0	21	164	450	716	725	616	487	180	34	0	3393

Mean percentage is the average amount of sunshine in an area

Degree Days is a rating of how much heating energy is needed by the average home in an area (higher numbers indicate a colder climate).

Notice, when you compare cities with similar latitudes, even though a city receives a higher percentage of sunshine, homes in that city may require more heating.

This greater angle means the suns rays have to pass through less of the earth's atmosphere, and the sun is visible for a greater number of hours during the day. As you move north, the angle of the sun decreases, and gets closer to the horizon.

The local weather conditions affect the available sun energy, by either allowing it to reach the earth, or by blocking the majority of the energy. The more clouds or storms you incur in your area, the less sunshine is available. The reduced sunshine results in less of the suns heat energy being available for you to utilize.

The amount of energy that reaches your location is important, because it determines how much heat your passive solar system can provide for your home. Because the local climate may prevent some solar energy from reaching your location on any given day, it is important to know the average percentage of sunshine available for your area when using a solar design.

This has been a brief summary of solar design and heating. All of these things can be combined to enable your home to capture some of the available solar energy, and to use it in place of fossil fuels, such as heating oil, natural gas, or propane. All of these fossil fuels are of limited quantity on our planet, and all of these generate some form of pollution as they are burned. Using solar heating to reduce fossil fuel usage reduces pollution released into our atmosphere, and helps to conserve our limited resources. There are many fine books that cover passive, and active solar heating design. These books generally contain information about the available solar heating potential in your area, as well as elaborate calculations about solar design. There are also professionals who have knowledge and experience in solar design. You should do your homework before setting out on any solar heating venture. Effective solar design can be accomplished by an amateur with an adventurous spirit, but this is not for the faint of heart.

Sources of information regarding solar heating are contained in the appendices of this book, and additional information can be found at www.futurehomestoday.com.

Afterword

There have been a great number of topics covered in this book. The focus has been mainly on the preliminary steps when considering the construction of a home. These may include the needs of the family, taking advantage of the building site, the construction methods and materials, and making use of the suns energy to heat the home. Many of the topics are not discussed in great detail but only touched upon in order to convey a general idea. There are many sources of more specific information. Some of these sources are listed in Appendix C.

The beginning of the book we dealt with what should be the basis for any house. These are building to suit our needs, not our egos, and staying within our budget so as not to add additional stress to our lives and those of our families. Building homes that will last several life times, not wasting the precious resources we have on our planet. Selecting building methods and materials with the idea of reducing our impact upon the land. Building homes that are energy efficient to further reduce the impact on the land and thus preserve it future generations. Building homes that do not adversely impact our health or that of our families. And lastly building homes that provide the safety and shelter our families deserve. Following these principles will help us better utilize the resources we have available.

The next chapter dealt with the building site of the home. There are many aspects of a building site which effect the cost of building the home and the comfort it provides the occupants after it is built. The differences between city and country living were examined. The orientation of the home with its surroundings and its orientation to the sun are also important to the comfort a home provides. The use of plants to provide privacy and energy savings are yet another item to consider when building a home.

The third chapter looked at the variety of building materials available today. Different building materials have different short term and long term impact upon the land and the environment. Some building materials have short life spans while other can last virtually forever. We discussed some alternatives to common building materials, and some building materials that provide energy savings in the finished home. What we build our homes of can have great impact on our environment today and that in the future.

The next chapter was about home construction methods. Discussed were the most common building practices, some of their shortcomings and some of their advantages. Also discussed were some alternative building methods, their advantages and disadvantages. Building practices can have as much or more impact upon the environment as the materials used to build the home. The building practices impact the energy efficiency of the home and the potential safety of the home. Building practices and building materials can also dictate how long the home will last.

The fifth chapter was about insulation, the various types of insulation materials used in homes, the energy efficiency of these materials, and how these materials are used. With most building methods, insulation is what adds energy efficiency to the home. Also discussed were the issues of vapor barriers, air infiltration barriers, and the need for ventilation in the home and the attic. The more efficiently we insulate and seal our homes, the more energy efficient they become. A more energy efficient home will have less impact upon the environment in terms of energy consumption.

The last chapter discussed passive solar heating. The sun is always shining. There is always solar energy available from the sun. This energy is perfectly clean and costs nothing to obtain and can cost very little to capture. Most homes built today do not take advantage of the heat energy from the sun. If we could get 30% to 40% of the heat for our homes from sunshine, we could reduce the amount of pollutants we add to our atmosphere by 30% to 40% on a daily basis. On a continual basis, the energy saved year after year, the energy savings and pollution prevention/reduction would be enormous. This alone could have a huge impact upon our environment.

In short, the choices we make for our homes impact our environment and our families, in the short term, in the long term, and in the future. Better choices today mean a healthier and better tomorrow. Consider some of these options and ideas as you think of building your next home. The next book in this series will deal with the design and layout of the home. More information on these subjects and others is available at www.futurehomestoday.com.

I welcome any suggestions, comments, or ideas you have regarding this book or its content. Please let me know of any informational or typographical errors you identify. All of these or anything else can be e-mailed to me at comments@futurehomestoday.com. Your input will be appreciated.

Thank you,

Appendix A

Questions to help you define your home needs:

What is your building budget?   _____

How long do you plan to live in your location?   _____

What is the probability of an employment relocation?   _____

How many people will live in your home today?   _____

How many bedrooms will be needed for these people?   _____

Are these people young children, teenagers, or adults?   _____

Do any of these people have special housing requirements?   _____

If so, what are they?   _____

How many people will live in your home in 5 years?   _____
    (include the probability of relatives)

How many bedrooms will be needed for these people?   _____

How many people will live in your home in 10 years?   _____

How many bedrooms will be needed for these people?   _____

Will any of the people above have mobility problems?   _____

Do any of these people have special housing requirements?   _____

If so, what are they?   _____

Do any of these people have health problems?   _____
        (respiratory problems, asthma, chemically sensitive?)

What kinds of spaces will be needed by the people living in the home?

_____   _____

_____   _____

_____   _____

_____   _____

Could any of these spaces serve double duty? _____

If so, which ones? _____ _____ _____

Do you want an open floor plan in your home? _____

Will you require spaces acoustically separated? _____

What type of privacy do you require? _____

What amount of security do you require? _____

What architectural features do you want in your house? _____

What outdoor areas will be included with the home? _____

What types of insects are common in your area? _____

Are these insects pervasive throughout the summer? _____

Will you need a screened area outdoors? _____

Will you be operating a business from your home? _____

Will people outside the family work in this business? _____

How many people from outside the family? _____

Will you require additional parking space for these people? _____

What is the water quality in your area? _____

Is the area prone to wild fires? _____

What are the chances of life threatening severe weather? _____

Our Home <u>Needs List</u>

Need	Want
_____	_____
_____	_____
_____	_____
_____	_____
_____	_____
_____	_____
_____	_____
_____	_____

Building Sites   Site Number _____

Address _____   Cost_____

Good (Pro)	Bad (Con)
_____	_____
_____	_____
_____	_____
_____	_____
_____	_____
_____	_____

Notes

_____

_____

_____

_____

_____

_____

_____

_____

_____

_____

_____

_____

_____

_____

_____

_____

_____

_____

_____

_____

Appendix B

Bibliography:
Below is a list of all books used as reference material in writing this book, information from periodicals and internet web sites not included.

Matts Myhraman and S. O. MacDonald. *Build it with Bales: A Step by Step Guide to Straw-Bale Construction.* Tucson, AZ.: Published by Out On Bale, 1998

Charles Woods and Malcolm Wells. *Designing Your Natural House.* New York, NY.: Published by Van Nostrand Reinhold, 1992

June Cotner and Steve Myrvang. *Home Design Handbook: The Essential Planning Guide for Building, Buying, or Remodeling a Home.* New York, NY.: Published by Henry Holt and Company, 1992

Sam Clark. *The Real Goods Independent Builder: Designing & Building a House Your Own Way.* White River Junction, VT.: Published by Chelsea Green Publishing Company, 1996

Edward Mazria. *The Passive Solar Energy Book: A complete guide to passive solar home, greenhouse and building design.* Emmaus, PA.: Published by Rodale Press, 1979

James Kachadorian. *The Passive Solar House: Using Solar Design to Heat & Cool Your House.* White River Junction, VT.: Published by Chelsea Green Publishing Company, 1997

Athena Swentzell Steen, Bill Steen, David Bainbridge, and David Eisenberg. *The Straw Bale House.* White River Junction, VT.: Published by Chelsea Green Publishing Company, 1994

Photo Credits:
All pictures not noted below are the property of John C. Clem.

pg. 17, Straw bale house, Greg Sands, Hill City, KS.
pg. 71, Rubber Roofing Shingles, Crowe Building Products, Ontario, Canada.
pg. 72, Straw bale house, Greg Sands, Hill City, KS.
pg. 73, Bamboo flooring, TimberGrass LLC., Bainbridge Island, WA.
pg. 85, Straw bale house, Greg Sands, Hill City, KS.
pg. 86, Straw bale house, Greg Sands, Hill City, KS.
pg. 87, Straw bale house, Greg Sands, Hill City, KS.
pg. 101, Polyicynene insulation, Icynene Inc.

Internet Site Reference   **Appendix C**

Below is a list of Internet resources for information and product manufacturers.

www.waterdata.com - get information regarding the quality of the water in your city.

www.eren.doe.gov - U.S. Department of Energy's home page for Energy Efficiency and Renewable Energy Network.

www.eren.doe.gov/millionroofs/ - U.S. Department of Energy's home page for solar energy promotion.

www.eren.doe.gov/solarbuildings - U.S. Department of Energy's solar buildings page.

www.epa.gov/iaq - EPA Indoor air quality home page.

www.epa.gov/iaq/radon - EPA Radon information page.

www.nrel.gov - National Renewable Energy Laboratory home page.

www.nrel.gov/surviving_disaster - National Renewable Energy Laboratory surviving disaster page.

www.ase.org/checkup/home/ - The Alliance to Save Energy's home energy checkup page.

www.solstice.crest.org - Solstice Internet site for sustainable energy.

www.homeenergysaver.lbl.gov - Energy saving suggestions from the Department of Energy.

www.cr.usgs.gov:8080/radon/radonhome.html - U.S. Geological Survey radon information page.

www.discoverit.com/at/phi/article.html - Radon information page.

www.alternate-energy.com - Alternate Energy Resource Index.

www.azstarnet.com/~dcat - Development Center for Appropriate Technology, straw bale resource.

www.txses.org/epsea/straw.html - El Paso Solar Energy Association, straw bale resource.

www.ntrma.com - The National Tile Roofing Manufacturers Association home page.

www.metalroof.org - Metal Roofing Association home page.

www.asphaltroofing.org - Asphalt Roofing Manufacturers Association home page.

www.bia.org - The Brick Industry Association home page.

www.cellulose.org - Cellulose Insulation Manufacturers Association home page.

www.concretehomes.com/welcome.htm - Portland Cement Association home page.

www.timbergrass.com - a supplier of bamboo products.

www.nsc.org/ehc.htm - National Safety Council, Environmental Health Center page.

www.nfrc.org - The National Fenestration Rating Council, window rating home page.

www.efficientwindows.org - Energy Efficient Windows Collaborative, Information about window technology and types.

www.oikos.com - Oikos green building source home page, information.

www.greendesign.net - Green Design Network home page.

www.builtgreen.org - Built Green Colorado, green building program home page.

www.sbicouncil.org - The Sustainable Energy Council home page.

www.its-canada.com/reed/iaq/index.htm - The Residential Indoor Air Quality Database (Canada) home page.

Updated Internet site listings are available at www.futurehomestoday.com.

There are many items you use everyday that can be, or should be recycled. These include waste items made of glass, plastic, or paper, but there are other items that should be recycled because of the potential for pollution they pose. Below is list of items and how they can be recycled. Most recycling services are free.

Unbroken glass containers - Most clear glass containers are recyclable, and are the most valued. Colored glass is almost worthless, and broken glass is very hard to sort. Containers made of ceramics, pyrex, window glass, light bulbs, and mirrors are typically not accepted for recycling. You do not need to remove labels from containers.

Newspapers - Most newspapers can be recycled. They should be placed in brown paper bags or tied with a natural twine. Newspapers for recycling should be kept dry to avoid contamination by water, dirt, or mold. Items that may arrive with the newspaper that are not recyclable include rubber bands or plastic bags. Do not bundle magazines with your newspapers, as they are recycled with a different process.

Mixed paper - Mixed paper from magazines, office paper, and photo copies can be recycled. Unacceptable items are waxed paper, milk cartons, carbon paper, laminated paper, neon paper, napkins, tissue, or any wet or food stained paper. Some recyclers will also accept corrugated cardboard and telephone books.

Metal cans - Most metal cans can be recycled many times. Do not recycle cans containing paints, cleaners, or other hazardous materials. You do not need to remove labels from containers.

Plastics - Some types of plastics are typically recycled, others are not. Plastics stamped #1, #2, or #4 can be recycled. Remove any liquids from the bottles, and check the container caps, they may be of a different plastic type; throw them away if they are not marked. Even a small amount of the wrong type of plastic in a batch can ruin it. This causes a large portion of recycled plastic to be sent to the landfill.

Motor oil - Used motor oil can be recycled or used as a heating fuel. Oil should never, under any circumstances, be dumped onto the ground or down a storm drain. Dumped oil will eventually contaminate water supplies in many areas. Most cities have free collection points for used oil, and many motor service businesses will accept your used oil for recycling.

Automotive batteries - Automotive batteries should be recycled at a qualified supplier in order to keep lead out of the environment.

142

Rechargeable batteries - Rechargeable batteries, such as Nickel-Cadmium (NiCad) batteries, should be recycled in order to keep cadmium out of the environment. Cadmium can pollute water supplies if these batteries are sent to a landfill. Rechargeable devices such as cordless telephones, power tools, or cell phones may use NiCad batteries. Alkaline and heavy duty batteries can be thrown away unless prohibited by local law.

Household wastes - Household wastes such as paint, pesticides, chemical cleaners, oils, etc. should never be sent to a landfill in liquid form, as they can leach into the ground and pollute ground water. These substances should be allowed to dry completely before sending to a landfill, or should be taken to a local hazardous waste site. Most cities provide this service for free.

Refrigerators, Heat Pumps, & Air conditioners - These items all use Chlorinated Fluorocarbons (CFCs) as a cooling agent. CFCs are know to cause deterioration of the ozone layer that protects the earth from the harmful rays of the sun. The CFCs from these devices should be removed by a professional and recycled as opposed to being released into the atmosphere. Many landfills and recycling centers offer this service for free.

More information is available at:

www. obviously.com/recycle/

www.futurehomestoday.com

A book that you may be interested in is: "50 simple things you can do to save the Earth"

Glossary

Air infiltration -The process by which outdoor air is allowed to enter the home through small gaps in the building/insulation materials. The outdoor air, being hotter or colder than the indoor air, reduces the thermal efficiency of the home.

Air infiltration barrier - Any material used to seal the outside shell of the home, reducing air infiltration. These are generally synthetic materials that allow water vapor in the walls to pass through the barrier, while preventing the movement of air.

Air-lock - A set of doors at the entry points of the home, designed to reduce air transfer as people enter or leave the home.

Radiant barrier - A reflective material installed below the roof rafters of the home, in the attic, and designed to reflect heat energy penetrating the roof, back toward the outdoors.

Heat recovery ventilator - A mechanical device installed in the home and designed to remove stale air from the home, replacing it with fresh outdoor air. This is accomplished while retaining a significant portion of the conditioning energy, heat or cold, from the indoor air, and transferring this energy to the fresh outdoor air being brought into the home.

Vapor barrier - A impermeable barrier, usually plastic, installed on the interior walls of the home, and designed to prevent the movement of water vapor in the home, through the walls, to the outdoors.

Sustainable architecture - The process of designing and building a home while utilizing building methods and materials that are resource renewable, produce minimal pollution in their manufacture and use, creating a structure that is energy efficient and long lasting.

Building green - See sustainable architecture.

Chemically sensitive - People whose bodies react adversely, illness or irritation, to chemicals present in their living environments.

Solar design - The process of designing a home so that it can take advantage of solar heat energy for heating purposes.

Double duty - Designing a room so that it can serve two or more purposes for the family, reducing wasted housing space, reducing housing costs, and making the home more efficient.

Electronic air filter - A furnace air filter that uses static electrical attraction to remove most airborne contaminates from the indoor air.

Media air filter - A furnace air filter made of a large piece of paper filter material, and is designed to remove most airborne contaminates from the indoor air.

Formaldehyde - A hazardous chemical used in many adhesives. Formaldehyde is slowly released, off-gassing, into the indoor air of a home as the adhesives age.

Advanced framing method - A method of wood stick-framing that uses less lumber to construct a home by using larger pieces of wood, and spacing those pieces further apart.

Life cycle costs - The total cost of the home, or building material in the home, from initial construction to end of life. Using life cycle costs can help justify the use of higher quality, longer lasting building materials in home construction.

Solar mass - A large mass of material (masonry, water, etc.) that is used as a heat storage unit and temperature buffer in a solar heated home.

Off-gassing - The process where materials release chemicals into the air as the material ages. Some chemicals released into the indoor air of a home can be harmful or irritating to people.

Volatile organic compounds - Organic materials that off-gas chemicals into the environment as they age.

R-value - The scale used to rate the efficiency of insulating materials. A higher R-value indicates a higher insulation value.

Summer solstice - The day of the year, June 21st, when the sun reaches its highest point in the sky, in the northern hemisphere.

Winter solstice - The day of the year, December 21st, when the sun reaches its lowest height in the sky, in the northern hemisphere.

Light spectrum - The total range of light energy, both visible and not visible. The light spectrum includes infrared light, visible light, and ultraviolet light.

Super insulated - The process of highly insulating a building, beyond common practices, with the intent of conserving heat energy.

Index